EVER PRESENT
PEACE

OTHER ENGLISH LANGUAGE
BOOKS BY ARNAUD DESJARDINS

The Jump Into Life: Moving Beyond Fear
ISBN: 978-0934252423
Hohm Press, 1994.

Toward the Fullness of Life: The Fullness of Love
ISBN:978-0934252553
Hohm Press, 1995.

EVER PRESENT
PEACE
Psychological and Spiritual Health

ARNAUD DESJARDINS

Translated from the French by Didier de Amorin

HOHM PRESS
CHINO VALLEY, ARIZONA

Cover Design: Becky Fulker, Kubera Book Design, Prescott, Arizona

Cover Photo: Christophe Boisvieux

Interior Design and Layout: Becky Fulker, Kubera Book Design, Prescott, Arizona

Library of Congress Cataloging-in-Publication Data

Names: Desjardins, Arnaud, author.
Title: Ever present peace : psychological and spiritual health / Arnaud Desjardins ; translated from the French by Didier de Amorin.
Other titles: Paix toujours prâesente. English
Description: Chino Valley, Arizona : Hohm Press, 2018. | Includes index.
Identifiers: LCCN 2018004357 | ISBN 9781942493396 (trade pbk. : alk. paper)
Subjects: LCSH: Peace of mind. | Spiritual life. | Self-realization.
Classification: LCC BF637.P3 D4713 2018 | DDC 204/.4--dc23
LC record available at https://lccn.loc.gov/2018004357

Hohm Press
P.O. Box 4410
Chino Valley, AZ 86323
800-381-2700
http://www.hohmpress.com

This book was printed in the U.S.A. on recycled, acid-free paper using soy ink.

This book was originally published in French by La Table Ronde, Paris, 2011.
www.editionslatableronde.fr
ISBN : 978-2-7103-6764-2

CONTENTS

FOREWORD

The Testament of a Spiritual Luminary

As he himself tells us in his introduction, Arnaud Desjardins (1925-2011) formally started his spiritual journey by joining the Gurdjieff groups in Paris at the age of twenty-four. At this time in 1949, Mr. Gurdjieff was still alive and though Arnaud never met him (he was to die this same year) his presence was very much felt in those groups led by his close associate and appointed successor, Madame de Salzmann. In my opinion, one cannot stress enough the impact of Mr. Gurdjieff's approach on Arnaud's future teaching. All the more so because Arnaud's guru, Swâmi Prajnânpad (189_-1974) whom he met in 1965, had in many ways a very similar approach, though he has never heard of Gurdjieff before and had a very different personality and way of life. When one reads Ouspensky's *In Search of the Miraculous,* which documents the early teachings of Mr. Gurdjieff, in parallel with Swâmi Prajnânpad's letters or recorded conversations with his disciples, the similarities are often striking, both in the ideas expressed and the vocabulary used. To give just two examples, both Gurdjieff and Swâmi Prajnânpad insist on the "mechanical" condition of the ordinary human being, imagining he is free whereas he or she is carried away and constantly "played" like a puppet by his automatic reactions. Both insist on one's inability to "do" and on the childish, immature state of one who has not consistently "worked." Hence the necessity of establishing "a doer" in oneself.

Living a secluded life in a small remote ashram in Bengal, Swâmi Prajnânpad was both a very traditional and atypical Indian Guru.

He was immersed in his Hindu heritage while also at times very critical of what he saw as its superstitious and "emotional" aspects. Very educated (a scientist by training, he had been a university professor), he was fluent in English, quoted Ruskin and Victor Hugo (whose *Les Miserables* he had read in English translation) and was an early admirer of Sigmund Freud. Far from the ashram crowds, he never welcomed more than two students at a time, to whom he gave private interviews every day and sometimes guided in a specific form of work on the unconscious which he had developed after realizing the emotional issues of contemporary seekers, both Indian and Westerners; he had nine French students in his late years, including Arnaud. He himself never wrote a book and lived in relative obscurity, but his teaching is now well known in the French-speaking world through his letters and transcriptions of his recorded talks with disciples. Famous philosophers are quoting him, and some tenets of his teaching have even made their way into psycho-spiritual best sellers, for better or worse.

Swâmi Prajnânpad's formulas, many of which have been collected by Veronique Desjardins in *Les Formules de Swâmi Prajnânpad* (La Table Ronde, 2003), are gems of concentrated and practical wisdom. The originality of these formulas lies in the fact that they manage to convey the essence of non-dual teachings as expressed by vedantic schools in very practical terms, immediately applicable in daily life. Though Swâmi Prajnânpad himself was a renunciate, the spiritual approach he taught is, like Gurdjieff's "Fourth Way," that of the human being fully immersed in the world. These formulas constitute the essence of Arnaud's teaching. He was, of course, deeply touched by his close contacts with many of the greatest spiritual figures of the twentieth century from different traditions: Tibetan and Zen Buddhism, Sufism, Hinduism—both Vedantic and devotional. Also, though very critical of his Protestant upbringing, Arnaud never rejected Christianity and the Gospels in particular, on which he wrote a fascinating book (*En Relisant les Evangiles,* La Table Ronde, 1990). All these influences are felt in his teaching, marked by its tolerance and insistence on the universality of the spiritual perspective in its essence, beyond religions and specific paths. Indeed, Arnaud, all his life and till his last days, was a tireless advocate of mutual understanding between different traditions, regularly inviting to his ashrams teachers and scholars from all paths.

I believe it is useful to point out one thing which Arnaud, in his modesty, could not himself mention: the huge impact he had on several generations of seekers in the French-speaking world, first as a filmmaker and writer, opening a whole new perspective to so many, then as a prominent and widely respected spiritual figure. For tens of thousands of readers and admirers, far beyond the numerous people coming to stay at his ashram, Arnaud Desjardins was the archetypal embodiment of "the sage," someone many looked up to. A lot of prominent writers and teachers regularly acknowledged their debt to him and felt honored to be invited to his ashram to speak and share.

A student of Arnaud since my early twenties, I had the privilege to write four books with him and to be one of his collaborators (teaching assistants) at his last ashram, Hauteville. (I was there on a permanent basis for eleven years, then as a regular contributor for the next ten years, including after his passing and up to this day.) I could of course say many things about Arnaud. Two strike me most in retrospect:

First, I believe that if Swâmi Prajnânpad was a genius in that, like all geniuses, he renewed his tradition and added a new element to it, Arnaud, for his part, was a pedagogical genius. He had an awesome talent for explaining and clarifying the highest teachings, as the present book clearly demonstrates. Secondly, I am awed by his dedication and active compassion. Arnaud literally gave his life to the teaching. With his reputation, he could so easily have led a rather comfortable and gratifying life, giving seminars, travelling here and there as a much demanded speaker. Instead, he chose to take on the huge responsibility of creating and animating on a daily basis a big ashram which he saw as both a place of possible deep work for those who had the motivation and as a more general place of nourishment and shelter for the many in need. In his eighties, Arnaud was leading the life of a forty-year-old CEO, bearing on his ample shoulders the weight of a multi-faceted task. To those of us who could see him at close quarters, he embodied the ideal of the Bodhisattva, forsaking his personal comfort for the sake of compassion. Prior to his last weeks, during which he was hospitalized, the very last morning of his life at his ashram was spent, as were most of his mornings, replying to his mail and then giving a question and answer session for about fifty people, during which he suffered a cardiac attack. As he was being helped out of the room, he turned one last time to his students and audience, reminding them that this was an opportunity to practice.

It should also be noted that Arnaud took great care in securing as much as possible what would happen after his passing. He trained teachers at his Hauteville ashram, trusting them, empowering them while never hesitating to give them lessons, sometimes hard ones. In his last years, he publicly and unambiguously appointed his lineage holder in the person of Eric Edelmann, who had been and still is in charge of Arnaud's ashram in Quebec: Mangalam, a place where he loved to stay and teach. He also gave every one of his close students his or her place in the transmission work, bestowing precious indications and directions many of us are still living from and assimilating. Today, his transmission lives on: at his ashram Hauteville, the responsibility of which now rests mainly on his son Emmanuel Desjardins, helped by a team of collaborators and staff; in his other ashram, Mangalam, led by Eric and Sophie Edelmann; and also in more informal, smaller structures through which students whom he empowered are carrying on in their own style and in alignment with the lineage. It should be noted that his wife, Veronique, while still contributing to Hauteville, is also teaching in her own style and carrying on his legacy. A circle composed of the students bearing a teaching responsibility has been meeting every year at Hauteville to deepen and nourish their mutual bond and commitment.

Ever Present Peace is in many ways the testament of a great spiritual teacher who had a unique and rare perspective, fed and matured by a lifelong commitment and his close associations with numerous spiritual giants. I would like to end this introduction by mentioning that it makes me very happy to see this precious book published in English by Hohm Press, founded by Lee Lozowick. Though outwardly so different, Arnaud and Lee were very close for nearly twenty years, sharing, from the day when they first met, a mutual admiration and spiritual communion which in itself constitutes a rare episode. Didier de Amorin, who has translated this book, is himself a long-time student of Arnaud and was also close to Lee, with whom he toured as a musician in a band uniting students of both schools.

May this book feed many hearts and souls.

—Gilles Farcet
Paris
May 2018

TRANSLATOR'S PREFACE

Arnaud has a golden heart.
—Swâmi Prajnânpad

I met Arnaud Desjardins' teaching in 1978 through a book called *Les Chemins de la Sagesse*. The three volumes that comprise it contain a wide presentation of the teaching that he received from his Hindu master, Swâmi Prajnânpad. With this reading, I had one clear goal in my existence: meeting the author, which I was able to do two years later. Since then, I have read the twenty books published under Arnaud's name, and over and over have come back to whatever chapter I needed to help me through any specific difficulty I met on my own path.

And then, when this one, *La Paix Toujours Présente*, was published I received a shock, a salutary one. After more than thirty years I was discovering at last what this entire teaching was about. Everything in it appeared clear and simple to me. *Yes...simple.* I didn't say "easy."

At the time of finding it—when it was just released—I felt a tremendous need for help, as I was going through a deep inner crisis, full of doubts and reactions toward Arnaud, my long-term master. So I was in an ideal condition to fully receive the message of this book.

Over time, after having read it again and again, and having studied each chapter point by point, what moved me the most was what I got at the level of the heart. Arnaud had clearly said, when he was in the process of writing this book, that it would be his very last one, his "spiritual legacy," so to speak. Knowing this, I could read between the lines his compassionate intention in writing it: "What can I tell my readers, my listeners, that they can get? How to put these teachings in the most understandable way? How can I *help* them in their thirst for peace and joy?" This realization brought me to tears and I understood then how deeply Arnaud loved me (and each one of us can say "me" here of course). He had made, once again, this effort to communicate the purpose of his whole life.

Although *Ever Present Peace* is focused on one specific teaching, which Arnaud gained from Swâmi Prajnânpad, it clearly has a universal value; it draws the reader back to the roots of *every* path, and to the fundamental aim of every spirituality: to be healed at last from suffering.

Although I am French, and reside in France, I have very good American friends—actually "brothers and sisters" who are committed to another spiritual lineage. Knowing their dedication to the Path, and their deep respect for Arnaud and his teaching, I felt a strong impulse to share with them the content of this inspiring, universal "treasure." And so began the work of translation.

Arnaud was always motivated by the desire for reconciliation among the different spiritual traditions. Rather than asking what divides these various approaches to the Path, his great interest was in "what is the *common* factor?" For this reason, in Hauteville, Arnaud's ashram in France, one will find *Beth David*, a Jewish study room, side by side a tiny Christian chapel, and next to a little mosque, and nearby a Tibetan Buddhist shrine room. Arnaud welcomed people from every religion as well as agnostics to his ashram. He said many times that, "if Hauteville can help a Christian, a Muslim, a Jew to be a better Christian, a better Muslim, a better Jew—someone who is able to really *apply* the fundamental teachings of their religions to their very life—then the ashram would have been of some use." Conversion was definitely not the point here. On the contrary, Arnaud cautioned his students from doing so.

Many wonderful books exist, from all around the planet, each containing many precious testimonies. Yet, sometimes these testimonies are hard to reconcile with those of other books, about other religions, other approaches, often because of the words in which they are expressed. Misunderstandings of the meaning assigned to various words has led even to wars. In meeting a spiritual teaching, therefore, we must be attentive to the meaning that the author assigns to each word.

Swâmi Prajnânpad, Arnaud's master, had a precise vocabulary in the communication of his teaching. While his vocabulary was not necessarily "better" or "worse" than another, it is important to understand the meaning of the words he used, in order that we can "translate" and hopefully reconcile his vocabulary with that of another approach.

For example: In this book, Arnaud speaks about "mind" and "ego." Yes, we have heard these famous words before, but still we must consider carefully what sense *we* attach to them as they are common and overused. The teaching that Arnaud Desjardins received from Swâmi Prajnânpad gives exact distinctions about these terms, and it will be beneficial to define them here at the beginning.

"Mind"—contrary to the ordinary understanding of this word as "intellect" or the "inner mood"—is, in Swâmi Prajnânpad's teaching, a translation of *manas* in Sanskrit, which roughly means "Liar." Mind/manas is a function whose purpose is to create illusions by distorting reality. Thus, based in this view, mind constantly affirms "this *should be* otherwise" (which conclusion gives rise to negative emotion). Or, "this situation *could have been* otherwise" (which generates the arising of positive emotion as I rejoice at my good fortune). The mind is opposite to neutrality: it affirms or rejects everything, and functions only by comparison.

The "mind" is to be distinguished from the "ego"—or more likely *the sense of* ego, of separateness—which, as an illusion, is a by-product of the mind. But ego by itself is to be seen as the remnant of the child in us, most of the time an unhappy and frustrated child, sometimes a deeply wounded one. The ego seen from this angle has to be considered seriously in order that it can, step by step, grow and enlarge itself—as Swâmi Prajnânpad would say, "ego has to get wider and wider so that it becomes eventually wide enough to contain the whole Universe". . . which means that it vanishes—"like a fruit naturally falls from the tree when ripe," in Arnaud's description. There is no longer any sense of separateness.

The mind's function is, on the contrary, to keep the ego narrow, shut down, and even to make it narrower and increasingly shut down. In Swâmi Prajnânpad's and Arnaud's teaching, the ego is definitely not the enemy of the seeker on the Path; the mind is the only enemy. And this enemy has to be fought with no mercy, but very skillfully—by not confronting it head on, especially at the beginning of the Path. But there is a "war" here, a very subtle one, but still a war. The mind is *manas*, the mind is the evil, Satan, the devil, *Sheitan* in the Sufi tradition, and the *jihad* (the spiritual struggle) has to take place exactly here.

Referring to the ego, Arnaud often used the image of the caterpillar, like Swâmiji did. The caterpillar is naturally drawn to a transformation, a dramatic one, that leads it to becoming a totally different animal that no longer simply crawls and feeds on leaves but is now able to move in a three-dimensional world, feeding on flower nectar. What a change! "More than a change actually: a transformation," as Arnaud puts it. We might imagine that this process—especially during the time within the chrysalis—is very scary for this poor caterpillar. In effect, the caterpillar "dies" to its previous form. The transformation "kills" the caterpillar. It is no longer able to recognize itself as it has always been: a quiet entity crawling around and living on leaves.

And Arnaud added sometimes: "Yes, the caterpillar has to become a butterfly but if you smash a caterpillar down [meaning, if you "kill" it before the transformation is complete] it won't make of it a butterfly but just a dead caterpillar!"

Similarly, one does not have to "kill the ego" in this teaching but "kill the mind"; and one has to learn how to discriminate one from the other by self observation, since ego and mind are intimately entangled. The Hindu tradition holds that the disciple has to develop discrimination to the same degree as the swan, which is supposedly able to separate milk from the water in which it is blended!

෨෬

With *Ever Present Peace* by Arnaud Desjardins we are in the presence of a precious source of wisdom, of inspiration on a Path toward peace and joy (would I dare to say "love"?) to the degree that we deeply reflect on the meaning of the words used by the author. From the depth of ourselves we must seriously consider what we are looking for...whatever the Path is that we are, or are not, committed to. And, even if one is not yet engaged on a Path, this book opens an accessible entry gate to understanding (or at least to catching a glimpse of) what spirituality is about.

Finishing this book was among the last projects Arnaud took on before his death. Using simple images, simple examples, he tried once again to touch our hearts for, as he would say sometimes, "the distance of the Path is actually very short, a few centimeters: the distance between the forehead and the heart." Another thing he used to tell all who approached him was: "This is possible for *you* ____!"— and there he added the first name of the person he was talking to.

Arnaud wanted us to be happy, no more, no less. This book, and the many insights and gifts of help I have received in the process of rendering it into English, has confirmed his intention for me once again.

—Didier de Amorin
St. Laurent-du-Pape
May 2018

INTRODUCTION

A long with the previous books published in my name, this one has
no philosophical or literary pretensions. The different chapters
that make it up have been delivered live before small audiences and
then transcribed from the recordings. It collects detailed answers
to questions asked by people committed, more or less long term, to
the Path of transformation that I have proposed since 1974. These
audiences, including Quebecers and Mexicans, were comprised
of men and women from extremely varied social origins, levels of
education, and age.

The teaching transmitted here is, above all, the result of nine years
of a personal search guided by the Hindu master Swâmi Prajnânpad
during my different long stays with him, plus about three hundred
interviews with him in the intimacy of his very small ashram. As
Swâmiji suggested, in the subsequent years I welcomed candidates
to wisdom who were interested in following the same Path that
I experienced myself. One other of his French students, Daniel
Roumanoff,[1] contributed to making him known and acknowledged
by a certain number of French intellectuals, thanks to the rigor of
Roumanoff's testimonies.

It's not obvious to me today what, in my understanding and my
experience, comes only from Swâmi Prajnânpad and what I owe to
other influences I encountered on my road. At the age of twenty-
four (in 1949), I entered one of the "Groups" directed by the direct
disciples of G.I. Gurdjieff: his recognized heiress, Madame de

---

[1]   Daniel Roumanoff was an acknowledged Sanskrit and Indian scholar.

Salzmann, and Henri Tracol. At this time, the audience for the study of spirituality was far different from that of today. And I could not have heard of this subject within a school of high political studies (from which I graduated in 1946).[2] All that I discovered within this Gurdjieff group about self remembering or "non-identification" with thoughts seemed to me totally new, even if it was, in fact, ancient knowledge retransmitted for centuries in a more or less pure and living way.

Starting in 1949, I fed myself with books, in French and in English, dedicated to esotericism, mysticism, and traditional doctrines coming from many origins like Hindu, Buddhist, Christian, Sufi, and the ancient Greek. Sixty years of reading now fills a library that becomes cumbersome at the end!

But if reading, re-reading, studying, assimilating a treatise of wisdom has its own part to play, nothing replaces meeting living witnesses. In 1958, one month in retreat at the Trappist Abbey of Notre Dame de Bellefontaine, and interviews with the abbot, the prior, and the master of the novices, opened me to a completely different understanding of Christianity and to a universe of old books that, because of my Protestant education, I had ignored. An unusual but deep and long-lasting friendship was born between the Reverend Father Dom Emmanuel and myself, which lasted until his recent death. I sometimes read that Arnaud Desjardins was a Hindu or a Buddhist. But I owe it to my experience at Bellefontaine for having been able to deepen my understanding of the message of the Gospel, rather than for my converting to another religion.

This being said, my explorations in 1959 of ashrams in India— those of Swâmi Shivananda, Mâ Anandamayi, Ramdas—and all the

---

[2]   Sciences Po (Political Sciences), the most prestigious French School in political matters.

Vedantic literature were for me, as also for my first wife, Denise, a tremendously moving revelation. Between 1959 and 1965, we divided our time between France (and the Gurdjieff groups) and India, following "Ma" in her tours, and living through, by our love for her, all kinds of discomfort and troubles. These trips were paid for by the films I shot in India and Afghanistan for the French Television, a public utility called O.R.T.F., which opened to a large audience a previously unknown world that I had discovered myself. Among the influences that motivate and inspire me today, I don't know exactly what I owe to Mâ Anandamayi, Swâmi Ramdas, and others, but what I do know is that I owe all of them.

During 1964-65, and again in 1967, I met His Holiness the Dalai Lama (at this time much more available than today) and the great Tibetan rinpoches from the first generation, refugees in India, who at that time had never traveled to the West—so many of them that I could not mention them all here. Having made movies under the Dalai Lama's supervision gave me the privilege of being accompanied and translated, during all these months, by his own senior interpreter, the Sikkimese Sonam Topkey Kazi, thanks to whom I could ask those masters very precise questions about the practice of meditation and thus confirm my own understanding. At the same period of time, I committed myself to Swâmi Prajnânpad, with whom I could talk directly in English. In our first ashram, "Le Bost," in the center of France, I welcomed Kangyur Rinpoche, Dilgo Khyentse Rinpoche, and the XVIth Karmapa. I know what the memories of each of them meant to me, and still mean to me overall. Their always-living presence remains a day-to-day inspiration; their imprint in me and their blessings have a main place in the background of what I may transmit and propose today.

Last, in 1967 and 1973, I spent several months in a country where I often stayed and shot footage, a place that I deeply loved— Afghanistan, which at this time was still peaceful and serene. Here

I studied with nearby remarkable Sufi *pirs*. I was accompanied and translated by a beloved Afghan friend, Mohammed Ali Raonaq. More than about technical matters (*Wazifa*, the *lataïfs*, purification of the *nafs*), so different from my own practices, my questions to these sages were about dualistic or non-dualistic metaphysics (*wahdat-al-shudud* and *wahdat-al-wudjud*), and the words of at least one of them were decisive in my own future orientation.

I must say that, whether I was near Hindu masters or Tibetan masters or *pirs*, my approach had not a university-like rigor. I noted down with much care some words and their comments, although I didn't precisely question about which Upanishad or which *hadith* of the Prophet in the Koran it came from. Regarding the Tibetan or Arabic or Persian terms, I transcribed them phonetically in order to be able to use them and deepen their meanings in the interviews to come. Furthermore, it's also true that this precision, of which I know the value—for I benefited from it myself as a reader of translated texts and comments—is not what the "seekers" I have met for the past thirty-five years have come to expect. All this is to clarify one point about the pages to come: they are only answers to human beings who feel that their existence cannot merely consist of succeed, fail, win, lose, be finally happy and then unhappy again, get old, and die.

This quest transcends time, cultures, races, religions. But whatever have been the betrayals of religions, the crimes committed in their names, and the hatred they created under the flag of the word "love," most of the time it has been within these various religions that minorities have lived and transmitted the most precious esoteric knowledge. Religions divide people, spiritualities unite them. I myself have never been able to see any differences between the peace, serenity, and love emanating from a mahatma, a rinpoche, a sheikh, or a Christian monk living in God.

This universal common background is behind the answers given in this book. Don't look for what you have no chance to find here;

that is, for a precise text including references and exact quotations. If you want to read a very well-constructed and detailed book, you can read the three volumes of *Les Chemins de la Sagesse,* and if you wish a technical Sanskrit vocabulary, you'll find it in the four volumes of *À la Recherche de Soi.* (Both series of books are only available in French to this day, published by La Table Ronde Editions.)

When *Les Chemins de la Sagesse* was published in 1968-70, I translated into French some English words (as well as those from other languages) that were used in a very specific way by Swâmi Prajnânpad. These were about striking ideas that I had at this point not read or heard anywhere else before. Swâmiji proposed to us several radical distinctions: between emotion and feeling, action and reaction, and thinking and seeing. So it was about not mistaking an *emotion* for a *feeling,* a *reaction* for an *action,* *thinking* for *seeing.* Those terms expressed deeply different realities which applied not just within one language. At the time, this choice of vocabulary provoked very critical reactions based on the assertion that these oppositions were not only arbitrary, but wrong. Today, forty years later, I have found these distinctions being used in books by recognized authorities.

So here is "one more book by Arnaud Desjardins that always says the same thing." Not *exactly* the same, and not *exactly* in the same way. And, as nobody has to learn by heart the whole content of every book of an author, it is not useless to hear again and again such truths as one can verify to the extent that these can transform one inwardly.

This book is like a series of letters addressed to a number of people: long letters written to some of those who are looking for help to transform themselves inwardly, to get free from their fear, and to establish themselves in the inner peace and love that have no contrary. There was a time when this kind of book had some originality. Today, many others are rooted in the more or less same background. But even if this kind of literature isn't subjected to any kind of restriction in France,[3] the idea itself of the master-disciple relationship is still highly suspect. May these pages help to pacify some worries about it.

To transmit a teaching—no matter which teaching, from medical training or photography to ice-skating—requires a specific vocabulary, including technical terms to which everybody gives exactly the same meaning. It should be the same in a school of wisdom, but it's far from that. Most of the time, the teaching is about doctrines that have been originally and very precisely expressed in languages other than French or English, such as Sanskrit or Pali, Hebrew, Arab, ancient Greek or Latin, Chinese, etc. Translations have varied according to the translators. The same term may be translated in our (the French) language as "soul," "spirit," or "consciousness." Sanskrit grammar, for instance, includes the neutral gender, in contrast to only two genders in French; thus, saying or writing "*le*" *brahman* (which is in French the masculine form of "the") gives already a certain "color." Neither Sanskrit nor Arabic have capital characters. In French,[4] certain words are more or less arbitrarily capitalized in books. Are words like *yoga* or *karma* Sanskrit words? Or are they French or English words coming from the Sanskrit? And these questions may be asked today about many other terms.

On the other hand, each tradition throughout history has been expressed in its own language, and each disciple, monk, or student relied only on this one language. Today, those who, for instance, knock at the door of our ashram in Hauteville have listened to conferences, read books, participated in seminars concerning a bunch of ideas from various origins. These people react positively to some words

---

[3] While Arnaud originally mentioned France in this example, the same is true in the U.S. and many other countries.

[4] Arnaud here refers to the French language, as this was the original language of this book. However, the same is true for English, and this practice is reflected also in this translated version.

that can sound bad or even painful and unbearable to others. The first and most well-known of these words—and the most variously interpreted—is the word *God*.

To talk about the "Ultimate Reality," which is the foundation of our individual *being* consciousness, everybody has his or her own favorite terms, and those that he or she rejects: God, the Absolute, the Infinite, the Eternal, the Divine, Atman (with the arbitrary capital character), or the Self (possibly the Supreme Self), Kingdom of Heaven which is inside of us, the Non-Born, Buddha Nature, true nature of the spirit, the Spirit (to distinguish from the soul), the Essence, and more. To take account of these differences I've been driven, even in the service of a precise teaching among others equally valuable, to use various terms as if they were synonymous. But I know, of course, to what extent they are not synonymous for a theologian. What is important when men or women come to us carrying their own existential difficulties, their sufferings, and their thirst for another quality of life is to show an actual possibility of Liberation in every human being—not to teach an academically correct doctrine.

And it's a fact that, if men or women who come to our ashram have no philosophical or theological preparation, some of them have already-, contrarily-decided convictions in this field. The common denominator for all of them is dissatisfaction (often an enduring suffering), along with hope for possible change and a longing for something more than psychotherapy. Ultimate, non-dualistic, metaphysical teaching, as it has been expressed as well by Hindu or Buddhist masters, is that, everything being evanescent, "there is neither creation nor dissolution; there is no slavery; no one to perform a spiritual practice; no one to look for liberation and no one to be liberated."[5] Path, practices, "heroic" efforts, improvements

---

[5]   Words to this effect are found in the "Heart Sutra," and in the teachings of Ramana Maharshi, among others.

are then only some aspects of the dream one has to wake up from. According to this radical view, all the pages that follow in this book would only concern the illusion of an ego who wants to reach what it already is. But this mirage would also apply to *asthanga marga* (the famous Eightfold Way) proposed by the Buddha. All of these practices that need perseverance appear, in this view, as weird as a user's manual for a wave that wanted to reach the ocean that *it already is*, in which *it remains* and *that remains in it* in the perfection of non-separation. In fact, in order for an ego (even illusory or unreal) to turn all its attention, its psychological energy, towards its source, towards the Self (*adhyatma*), one needs a powerful and united energy free from the usual thoughts, emotions, desires, and fears (*vasanas* and *sankalpas*).

In one sense, all that is told or described in the chapters to come concerns a preparation for a direct, deep dive into the depth of Consciousness. Each reader will have to discover if his or her own experience expresses itself according to classical images: like the drop of water reaching the ocean; like the full water jar that breaks when immersed in the sea, thus eliminating all separation; or like the river that, although having reached the ocean, still continues to flow towards it.

CHAPTER 1

RECOVERING FROM
SUFFERING

Jesus said, "I didn't come for the healthy, but for the sick" (Luke 5: 31) and, among other names, Buddha has been called "the Great Physician." One may forget, at least for now, great terms like *awakening, liberation, enlightenment,* and use the word "recovery" as a base.

Recovery and physical health depend on doctors and surgeons—on diagnoses and therapeutics. Even unversed in the matter, we all know what health is about. Persisting cough, disorganized cardiac rhythm, painful rheumatism, these are all symptoms we want to suppress. When all pathological symptoms are gone, then comes basic health.

Psychological health depends on psychiatrists, psychologists, and psychotherapists. A precise, professional vocabulary defines and describes different pathologies. The healing process is considered through chemistry (anxiolytics or anti-depressants), or through an intervention to the psychological program itself. Psychotherapy doesn't mean recovery *of* the psyche but *by* the psyche, the first and most representative example being Freudian psychoanalysis.

But what about spiritual recovery and perfect spiritual health? Two formulas have gained a certain fame: Psychotherapy heals the ego, spiritual practice heals from the ego; and Psychotherapy heals the mind, spiritual practice heals from the mind. In fact, all that is not intimate peace—unalterable, non-dependent joy and love with no contrary—is pathological from the spiritual health point of view. For four millennia, traditional descriptions of the saint or the sage are unanimous about this. Christianity promises a "peace that surpasses all human understanding" and a "perfect joy." The terms *shanti* (peace) and *ananda* (joy) saturate Sanskrit literature. Each one may honestly and realistically ask themselves where they are in regard to this, no matter what "spiritual experience" or moments of "supra-consciousness" they may have had.

Perfect spiritual health is in no case a guarantee of physical health. If some yogis may have had extraordinary physical health even when very old, most of the greatest sages got sick in old age. The difference was in the way they lived with these troubles and in their testimonies of awakening or Liberation in an extraordinary way through the ruin of their physical bodies. Also, don't mistake psychological health for spiritual health. Even if every sage and saint throughout the centuries always agreed about spiritual health, about psychological health we can see many disagreements, even among experts, regarding what is considered as "normal" and what is not, no less about the state of the inner emotions and external behaviors.

For some psychiatrists or psychoanalysts, spiritual research itself is considered as pathological. I've known two psychoanalysts who took a very clear stand: We know that the healing process is over when the patient recovers from all interest in spiritual life. They considered spiritual life as an escape from the hard reality of life (which it is sometimes), and even absolute serenity in the midst of trials was seen as an absolute form of denial, a shift in the form of compensatory delirium. (I can think of at least one very precise example of this.)

Buddha said, "I only teach two things, O disciple, suffering and cessation of suffering." People have often accused the Buddha of pessimism. In the past, I have read pages and pages of the works of Christian authors who opposed this Buddhist pessimism with the joy promised by Jesus Christ. But, in fact, I noticed more joy among Tibetan Buddhists, even as refugees in very hard conditions in India, than among many French Christians.

Buddha's awakening is, in a large part of Asia, as important as the resurrection of Jesus on the morning of Easter for many Christians. It is an event that concerns the whole universe, and, according to the Buddhist legend, the gods themselves in every subtle kingdom were amazed with wonder. But the "Perfect"—this being one of Buddha's names—says: "What I discovered is so far from the usual preoccupations of men, so different from all their convictions, that it won't interest anyone. Nobody will understand what I could say."

Tradition tells that a god of the pantheon said that if you speak, many won't listen, will criticize you, and will laugh at you; others will find it very interesting and will forget it immediately. But a few will listen, will be convinced, will practice and will reach awakening too (which sounds pretty similar to the Parable of the Sower in the Gospel). But the Buddha declared: "Well, for those ones I will turn the wheel of the Dharma; I will attempt to teach what I understood and to show the way."

He decided first to find the old companions he had during his years of austerity—those who had turned away from him when he ceased mortifications and accepted a bowl of rice with milk offered by a young woman. The Buddha then went to a park near the town now called Benares (or Varanasi) that already existed three thousand years ago: the park of Sarnath, the park with deer. His former fellow students, seeing him from far away, decided to greet him politely with a mere gesture of the head, but when the Buddha came closer, the light that emanated from him was such that the four *sadhus* bowed down, forehead to the ground. Then the Buddha opened his mouth for the very first time since his enlightenment. It was as if the whole world suddenly stopped. Buddha was about to teach the Truth. And he pronounced these famous words: *sarvam dukkham*, "All is suffering." Existence is mostly suffering. Painful circumstances are cruel and hurtful, and happy circumstances are disappointing, for they never last forever. A short moment of happiness cannot be complete, for we well know in the depth of ourselves that it will not last. The joy of a birth carries in itself the pain of a mourning.

Buddha spoke the Truth. Under infinitely renewed forms, suffering rules the world. There are those who lie on hospital beds with tubes, wires, perfusions; with more or less serious symptoms. There is the pain of seeing children suffering; of professional worries; of difficulties between children and their parents; of violence and wars...and so on—to say nothing of the greatest personal tragedies. It's not enough to live with the idea that it will get better later— tomorrow I will succeed; tomorrow I will meet true love; tomorrow I will be really happy—to settle into serenity and joy. *No.* Suffering rules the planet.

And Buddha continued: "To be separated from what one loves is suffering; to be united to what one does not love is suffering." It's so obvious! Coming into this world is suffering. Twenty-five hundred years after Buddha, we recognize the trauma of birth. It's a brutal shock for the baby to leave the peace he was in when in the maternal uterus. Sickness is suffering, getting old is suffering, and one is fighting today to discover "anti-age" creams. Death is suffering—to those who are afraid to die, and to those who have lost a beloved friend or relative.

Of course there are happy times, but they fool us. During my thousands of meetings with people for over thirty-five years, they never simply said, "I'm very happy." Everybody expressed one form or another of uneasiness, if not distress. Sure, there are times when a happy emotion comes when there is good news, but this emotion, depending entirely on the circumstances, doesn't last for long. Yes, from time to time we've been joyful; yes, we hope we'll find happiness tomorrow. But most of the time it is, If only things could turn out this way, then I would be fulfilled, or When I am successful in this or that, then it will be wonderful. "If" and "when." Yet, in a session with a Tibetan Rinpoche someone at age thirty will talk of their suffering, and twenty years later, when they meet a Hindu sage, they will talk again of their suffering. I'm not being morbid in saying this. I see it in my everyday work.

There *are* actually joyful moments—and you'll be able to appreciate them insofar as you change within—but still, fears concerning the future don't disappear. So, here is the important statement: Neither improvements in the medical area, nor education and public schooling for all, neither democracy nor socialism, nor liberalism, nor improvements in the sciences...nothing has made existence less tragic. I'm not saying this in a desperate and depressed way, but still I say it, feeling intensely all this suffering that I'm listening to and have welcomed for many years and thinking of all those who suffer everywhere in the world, in towns and villages, even where I've never been.

Fortunately, the Buddha's testimony doesn't stop there. He promises that there is something beyond the suffering. My own conviction is not that we have to convert ourselves to Buddhism, but that we have to see that this approach is universal. There is something to be discovered that is on a completely different plane from all of our usual experience that implies much more than an improvement regarding our ordinary way of seeing things.

In his famous first discourse at Sarnath, Buddha, having said, *sarvam dukkham*, "All at the end is deceptive," then adds, "There is one cause of suffering."

What? *One* cause of suffering? There are thousands of reasons to suffer, so many ways to be separated from what one loves, or united to what one doesn't love. In our usual experience, there are unlimited types of suffering: sickness, mourning, lack of money, aggression, abandonment, treason, misunderstandings between husband and wife, people speaking badly about us or malevolently to us. Our mind is absolutely convinced that if I'm unhappy, worrying, anxious, it is because of this or that. And that is what everyone who has been coming to me for so long shares about.

Yet, Buddha really said there is *one* cause, and this one cause is not external to us. There are millions of apparent external reasons for suffering, and we will never be able to remedy all of them. If we are able to heal one sickness, a new one appears; one may improve one's financial condition, but then one worries about the elder son who takes drugs; and so on, whatever the plan be, individual or collective.

What can we understand when Buddha teaches that there is only one cause to so many different sufferings? That this cause is *in us*! In our way of perceiving, conceiving, and qualifying things. Everything about this subject is communicated with the three words *perceive*, *conceive*, and *qualify*. I perceive something and I draw this conclusion: This is very good news. This makes me happy. This is my conviction for now. Then I perceive something else and I find it threatening. Whether I decide that it is happy or it is worrisome, this is all my idea; it is me who sees it this way. And, in the face of every occurrence, Buddha dares to affirm that there is only one cause of suffering: It is in you. It depends on the way you feel and conceive of every event, each situation, each phenomenon. This is a highly developed topic in the Stoic school.

If you make the effort to study different traditions, you will find this teaching everywhere. It is exactly the same as Swâmi Prajnânpad's. And Christ never said, Thanks to my words the world will be so transformed that there will be only happiness on Earth. He said, "In the world ye shall have tribulation; but be of good cheer, for I have overcome the world." (John 16:33)

Buddha's teaching is extremely precise, almost scientific: *There is one fundamental origin to suffering.* This affirmation is the second of what are translated in English as the Four Noble Truths.[1]

The Third Noble Truth is that if you eliminate this origin, you eliminate suffering. The Buddha did not teach that you eliminate the causes of suffering on Earth, but that you eliminate the fact of suffering itself. It is clear, even if astonishing. You may not believe it right away, but this teaching has produced extremely convincing results for twenty-five hundred years, and it is compatible with every other genuine spiritual approach.

The Fourth Noble Truth is that there is a way, a method, which eliminates suffering by eliminating its cause. This is the core of the Path. If you can reduce your own unpleasant circumstances, do it. If the bank refuses you a loan, try another bank. And if you have a headache, take aspirin. In India, one would never consider administering morphine to a *jivan mukta* like Ramana Maharshi, who was in much pain with cancer of the shoulder. But one of his long-term and elder disciples told me that one day the Maharshi said to him, "I have headache, give me some aspirin."

This apparently casual and ordinary story had a deep impact on my existence. What a simple way of acting! On the pain of the cancer, I can do nothing, and aspirin would be of no effect. But, on the headache, aspirin can be useful. I considered this demand from Bhagavan Ramana Maharshi as an immense teaching.

This being said, when we are no longer completely selfish, we wonder how we could diminish not only our personal painful

---

[1]   The First Noble Truth, *sarvam dukham*, as Arnaud has previously noted, is expressed as: "All life is suffering."

situations but also those of others, in various and more or less efficient ways. One cannot say that Communism, which represented an immense hope to a part of humanity, much reduced the suffering among the Russian people. Whether we speak of collective tragedies or intimate distresses, what people have always tried to do was to change the innumerable factors, even through violent actions that led to new tragedies. Of course, acting in order to relieve and help those who are crushed by existence is right, but it is an answer that will always be limited.

So Buddha said, the cause is in you. There are thousands of external causes, but only one inner cause. You will not eliminate all the external causes of suffering, but you can eliminate the feeling of suffering itself. From this angle there is a very simple truth, but we have to integrate it fully in order that it need not be discussed anymore. When one says, "My God, so many sufferings in this world!," what is one exactly talking about? Trials, tragedies, a tsunami, a civil war? Or is it about the intimate experience—sometimes horrible—of men, women, and children who unfortunately are anxious, tortured by their own painful emotions? In general, the same word—"suffering"—is used from both angles. And *it is possible* to discriminate between them. It is possible that situations that have been painful for so long do not have to hurt you anymore. In other words, it is possible that you may discover forever, within yourself, a peace, a joy, a serenity, a safety, an absence of fear that does not anymore depend on conditions, circumstances, events. This fundamental idea inspires the whole Path. But at the beginning of the Path we have almost no idea what I am talking about here. We only know that what we call "good news" makes us happy and that what we call "bad news" makes us unhappy. And, to us, there seems an unavoidable cause-effect relationship. But, in fact, you *can* stop it; you *can* stop the power that events have over you, which steals your peace, your joy, your availability for love and compassion.

So the good news is that there is one origin, a single one, to every form of suffering, and *that this origin is in us*. If it were outside, there would be no hope, for we have very limited power over the outside. But inwardly you will discover immense possibilities. If there *were* an unavoidable cause-effect relationship, I could not call it an "official" or "seeming" cause of suffering. Instead, I would say *the* cause of suffering.

If I were to take a wooden stick and hit Mâ Anandamayî with it, or Ramana Maharshi, or Kangyur Rinpoche, all of them would develop hematomas; it is an inexorable causality law. But if, after the invasion of Tibet by China, Kangyur Rinpoche, having lost all, finds himself in India not speaking a single English word, with several children, including one sick son, and no money, here are many reasons to be desperate. Yet I met him...radiant with serenity, sublime, unforgettable, completely available to others. In his case the cause-effect relationship was not at play anymore. So, too, if you say something extremely unpleasant to someone who functions in an ordinary way, you "hurt" him or her. Say something even worse and threatening to Kangyur Rinpoche, Swâmi Ramdas, or Swâmi Prajnânpad and you absolutely do not hurt them. And you do not affect at all their love for you.

Through these observations we get closer to the understanding of the Four Noble Truths stated by Buddha concerning the mechanism itself of suffering. If you eliminate the inner cause, you do not eliminate the concrete causes of suffering; this is another topic. But if you uproot the intimate germ, the tribulations of existence will not have the power to make you unhappy anymore. To say it this way is to express it in a simple and realistic way. But all of us, when we start on the Path, look for obvious outer justifications for suffering. And we are totally at the mercy of these justifications—so we are one moment joyful, one moment desperate, depending on the day-to-day circumstances. Our idea is always: How will I eliminate or at least diminish the external causes to my suffering?

Even after several years of commitment on the Path, one can well see that, for many, the questions persist about how to change the situations that are responsible for my discomfort. Even the idea of a change in your being is completely connected to the hope that this change will modify the outer conditions. If I change, if I become better, I will get more success professionally. Or, Women will be more interested in me. And you will always put your hope—for being free from suffering, free from fear, in the end happy at last—into the improvement of all kinds of circumstances.

Observe, verify for yourself: Can I be okay with such ideas? These *hopes* attached to situations are to the detriment of the real *Hope*.[2] We have all kinds of hopes: earning more money, a new medicine due to medical research that will cure my illness...thousands of hopes. *If only this could happen. Ifs* and *whens* play the game of the mind. There are thousands of hopes, so many, but there is only one Hope, a single one: *Eliminate in yourself the root of suffering so that external conditions, even adverse ones, will have no power anymore over your peace and your inner intimate serenity.*

Even if you can hear and accept this principle intellectually, you cannot be thoroughly convinced. So you will continue to put many expectations into your hopes, forgetting that this Hope proposes an aim different from every ordinary aim—that is, of uprooting within ourselves the possibility of suffering itself. Not suffering as a painful event, but the suffering that is an internal emotional experience.

With a bit of research you will find, fundamentally, the same teaching about suffering in Christianity, which promises us "a peace beyond understanding," and a "perfect joy." Yes, for two thousand

---

[2]   In French we have two words to express this difference: *espoir* and *espérance*.

years there have been descriptions of saints who, in the worst conditions, were radiant with peace and joy. It is incomprehensible, yet true. So don't say this understanding is only found in Buddhism.

The great question for you, the most important question on the Path actually, is: *What is this sole cause within me?* Sages will answer you, "It is the ego," or "It is the mind," for there are different ways to describe this sole psychic cause. Circumstances that would have hurt you before...there will always be some. But making it possible that these circumstances cannot affect your serenity anymore, leaving you free from fear, this is the profound core of all religions.

Jesus said, "My Kingdom is not of this world." (John 18:36) It doesn't depend on good news or bad news. If one reads the Gospels, one must remember that the most important issue for every Jewish person at the time was an external situation. Israel was colonized, enslaved by Romans—strangers, conquerors, pagans. Then Jesus dared to say about a Roman centurion, an idol worshipper and an invader of the territory, "Even in Israel I never saw such a faith." (Matt. 8:10)

Just for words like these Jesus could have been killed by stoning even before all that led to his being crucified. So if one reads the Gospels attentively, one understands that the most important thing for Christ was not to change the external situations. "My Kingdom is not of this world," but you may discover It in this world...and so many Christian saints have proved this.

Many Sufis throughout history have been persecuted by narrow-minded orthodox Muslims. Still—every testimony says it—they praised the Lord, they blessed those who tortured them. This isn't only Buddhist teaching. It is the very core of the Path. The cause of our suffering, the possibility of suffering itself, is in us; it is in the egocentric way we function. And about your inner world you *can* do something; you can even do much. These affirmations are not Buddha's thoughts or Swâmi Prajnânpad's ideas, they are truths that are transmitted by every sage recorded in the earliest testimonies, for three or four thousand years. And the more one frees oneself from one's emotions and fears, the more one is available to welcome others and to attempt to help them within the limits of one's possibilities, and within the non-limits of one's love. It is to this fundamental Hope that this entire book is dedicated.

☙

The Path (*marg*) was shown by Buddha, but is not exclusive to Buddhism. The differences and contradictions among various traditions are mostly about the vocabulary used. One may, for instance, demonstrate the similarity (and not the opposition) between the *atman* from the Vedanta and the *Non-Born* from Buddhism, both of which reveal themselves when ego vanishes.

The essence of the Path is self-knowledge that leads to Self knowledge. What Buddhism indicates as "the true nature of spirit" is called, in translations from Hindu Sanskrit, "the true nature of Consciousness," free from identification with always changing "forms" (sensations, emotions, thoughts). And our intimate transformation, the liberating experience, is before all else the fruit of this true "self knowledge." And Saint Augustine declared, "If I knew myself I would know You."

Except as a dead body, a human being is not a fixed object—like a skeleton or some piece of furniture—but a functioning nonstop *process*. Chemical and electrical phenomena are going on and on, asleep or awake. Yes indeed, modern scientific research, thanks to more and more efficient instruments and apparatuses, has taken the knowledge of emotional and cerebral mechanisms extremely far. But by a process of self consciousness and self observation, with an intensity that contemporary Westerners cannot figure out, the Ancients who originated these different esoteric teachings precisely spelled out and transmitted another type of knowledge, also extremely rigorous, precious, and overall liberating.

One can find, for instance, an aspect of this knowledge in the Buddhist doctrine of the five *skandhas: rupa, vedana, samjñana, samskara,* and *vijñana,* terms that are generally translated as form, sensations, conceptions, formations (or inductive tendencies), and consciousness. But reading about these terms merely out of one's commitment to a qualified Buddhist master is not enough to give one a clear experience of the fundamental process that all of this is about.

A simple approach, independent of Buddhist orthodoxy, is summarized in the use of five terms: *perception, conception, qualification, impulse* (or propensity to act) and *action* itself.

Generally, the *perception* is objective. Most of the time we see and hear in much the way that a movie camera "sees" and records—and it is the same for the other five senses. I am talking about perception of our current day-to-day existence, not taking account of ultra- or infra-wave lengths, which can be perceived or not by our eyes or ears. Nor am I speaking of possible pathologies.

Then comes *conception*: This is an armchair. That is a telephone ringing...a smell of gas...etc.—or thoughts about more complicated situations, more or less fraught with consequences. But the perception itself is sometimes already wrong. For instance, we are sure, certain, to have heard something that was not there. Sometimes what follows after the experience, or after an explanation by others, can show us our mistake; however, sometimes our mental conviction remains the same. A particularly famous example is of a piece of rope lost in a field that, in the shade, we mistake, at least in India, for a snake. All of this is easily explainable and simple to understand, but existence—with its fears, its sorrows, its sufferings, or its euphoric moments—makes the present reality appear to you much more complex and confused, and will require from you an exceptional quality of attention to clearly see what it is about. Try, nonetheless, to observe not only how *others* function around you, but also how *you* function yourself.

If, most of the time, *perception* is objective (or relatively objective) and shared with others, *conception* will be more or less subjective and will depend on personal interpretation. A native from a tribe totally ignorant about the modern world (if there are still some) who perceives a surgical operation would conceive it as a torture practice, a ritual sacrifice, or a murder attempt. Do not let such an unusual example turn your attention away from your own observations in the midst of your personal existence.

After *perception* and *conception*—or *rupa* (Sanskrit, meaning "form") and *nama* (meaning "name"); also "the world of *nama rupa*"—comes *qualification*: Something is good or bad, and every nuance is either beautiful or ugly, reassuring or threatening, noble or shameful, praiseworthy or guilty, etc. With *qualification* we enter the vast field of opinions and judgments, the most contradictory ones, the domain in which everyone lives in his or her own world.

As a contemporary example, *perception* will notice a doctor working on a female patient, *conception* will distinguish that it is an abortion (I "name," *nama*, what I "see," *rupa*), and *qualification* will be totally contradictory, depending upon whether the observer is a progressive atheist or a convinced Catholic, to say nothing of the differences of sensitivities according to the fact that the witness is a man or a woman.

After *qualification* comes *impulse* (propensity to act): to intervention in circumstances, with all the various and contradictory ways that can happen, depending on the emotional background of one or another. This propensity or intention (*sankalpa*) is, or is not, put into *action* according to externally favorable or unfavorable conditions and to the degree of inner division present within the person—i.e., you.

This mechanism of *perception*, *conception*, *qualification*, *impulse* and *action* (or non-action, which is the passive form of action) is unceasingly at play, in various degrees, in each one of us...each one of you. It is through this mechanism that we are happy or unhappy. This mechanism may be lived more or less consciously and lucidly. It is more or less enlightened by awareness, by presence in oneself and to oneself, here and now...and all the similar terms connected with it.

To summarize what this is about, and which I insist concerns all of you all the time, I will use a particularly well-known example from the psychological and therapeutic field: that of a little child who surprises his parents in the act of making love. His or her *perception* is the same as that of a cameraman who shoots an erotic movie. Daddy and Mommy are embraced; Dad is on Mom and moves a lot; Mommy is moaning and then gives out a long scream. The child's *conception*, contrarily, will undoubtedly not be: My parents are lucky, they are having good sexual intercourse. But rather: Dad is hurting Mom; he is brutal to her. *Qualification* will be obvious: This is wrong. *Qualification* by a psychotherapist, however, seeing the same scene, and whose everyday job is about sexual frustration among couples, would be, contrary to the child's impression, seeing in it absolute good!

Then comes, in the child, an impulse, a propensity to *act*: I will protect Mommy against Daddy. And also probably an inhibition to act this way because of fear. The final action will perhaps be to run away. Knowing what the trauma was and what kind of therapy will be able to heal the child is not the question here. You have here a clear illustration of the way things function and reign over our existence and a key to better understanding the essential difference that Swâmi Prajnânpad made between *mechanical reaction* and *deliberate action*, which is the appropriate response that the situation requires.

As recognizable as this example of a wrong interpretation may be, it has the disadvantage, first of all, of making you uneasy due to its crudity, and overall seeming to you as being far, far away from your daily life. Yet this error in *conception* and *qualification* plays a much more important and serious part in our personal history than we agree to admit. There are *situations*, and mind makes *problems* of them. From something good comes something bad; from something bad results something good. But we come to conclusions about such things too quickly. We worry or rejoice too soon. Only objective and persevering observation of your most subjective functioning will allow you to come to certainty for yourself about that, and give you a convincing experience of the shocking formula offered by Swâmi Prajnânpad that "No one is living in the world; each one is living in his or her own world."

❧

I often quote the Hindu formula that, *I may doubt everything, but I cannot doubt the one who doubts.* This idea concretely helped me in the past. In fact, it is astonishingly close to a famous saying in Western culture: *Cogito ergo sum*, by Descartes. "I think; therefore I am." Descartes wrote that he may doubt the existence of all he can see around him, but he cannot doubt the fact that he thinks that he doubts. To be able to think that he can doubt everything, there must be a thinker. It is because I think, that I know that I am. Yet the Hindu formula is about the one who doubts, and not the one who *thinks* that he or she doubts. This distinction, using the word "who," comes from the French and English translations, but in accordance with the Vedanta spirit, we'd better use the neutral form, "this." It is *this* that doubts.

These precisions are useful, for they focus on an essential theme of self knowledge—the relationship between the thinker and the thoughts. There only is a thinker when he or she is thinking, and thoughts are a flow, a succession, a non-stop change. The thinker is, in no case, a permanent "I am." But immutable Consciousness underlies this flow, this movement of a mechanical set of gears. And about *that* the Western reader meets with difficulty, relative to the different meanings one gives to the term "consciousness." This term is not the same in today's available translations into our languages (French or English) from Buddhist or Vedic literature, to say nothing of its definition in philosophical or psychological vocabulary.

I will only consider the Sanskrit term *chit* that points to this fundamental reality (not to be mistaken for *chitta*: the psyche, including memory and the unconscious). By itself, chit is involved neither in time nor in space, nor in causality, nor in any kind of measure (whatever the unit of measure may be), nor in attraction and repulsion. It is this supra-individual Consciousness that one may have a glimpse of in the "interval between two thoughts," about which Yoga as well as Vedanta have so insisted. From this view, "I think" involves: I am only change, impermanence, not the slightest fixed entity. Truth then is: I think; therefore I am not. It is *asat*, the non-real. *Asato ma sat gamaya*. From unreal, lead me to real. Make me discover the immutable and permanent *atman*.

Of course, those considerations may appear specious and far removed from your worries, from your difficulties, from your "problems," and from your hopes. And yet they are the bases of what you call the "Path" or the "Way" towards the end of suffering. Once again, if you do not know precisely which meaning and content you are giving to the terms *consciousness*, *soul*, *spirit*, *thought*, *mind*, *me*, *I*, *ego*, *sensations*, *emotions*, and *feelings*, you are, in your day-to-day practice and your progress, in the same situation as an electrician who gives more or less imprecise meanings to the words *watt*, *ampere*, *volt*, *tension*, etc.

So you can already follow further on your investigation into the true meaning of the term *consciousness*. If you—meaning your physical body—are at the train station in Valence, France, the city of Paris is already a simultaneous reality; from a satellite the two towns are perceived at once, not separated by time. To your physical body, the distance in miles will be experienced as a *duration* of the trip (yet shorter by train than by horse riding, but shorter in the past than by foot). You go onto the car you reserved a seat in, the TGV-train[3] starts, and through the window you see the landscape passing four times faster than it was in the steam trains of my childhood.

The perception of the TGV travelling, as well as the movement of your body towards the buffet car where you go to have coffee, appears to you, in the field of your consciousness, as a succession of events. But can you say that the "conscious," in itself and by itself, is situated in space or in time? It is...that's it...*sat* (being) and *chit* (Consciousness), infinite and eternal. The whole trip unrolls inside Consciousness, in the field of Consciousness. Consciousness does not move. Of course the physical body is always situated at one point in space and at one point in time, but time and space appear in the infinity of Consciousness. It is not "you," in the ultimate meaning of "I" or "I am," who makes the trip; it is *in you* that the travel is made. This is not intellectual juggling but a possible realization, available to the ascetic, to the yogi—and why not to you?—about which we have testimonies coming from three thousand years and more before TGV. But never mistake *Consciousness* for *the conscious* in relation to the unconscious.

Do not forget that in 1905, when Einstein published his discoveries that changed the world, he did not work in a laboratory with very sophisticated instruments and surrounded by prestigious collaborators. He was merely an employee in an office, having

---

[3]   Train à Grande Vitesse (very high speed train).

only the brain of a genius at his disposal. Cannot we admit that three thousand years ago other genius brains—*rishis*, as one says in India—discovered and transmitted astonishing truths to the ordinary brain?

This infinite Consciousness has been spoken of in various ways in different languages, but all point to the ultimate depth in ourselves, towards the Divine or metaphysical Source of our individual consciousness, although it is submitted to suffering and fear. It is the ignorance of this truth about yourself that is the cause of all your frustrations and all your anxieties. Uprooting the cause in order to uproot suffering from our hearts is to liberate oneself from the limited consciousness (the narrow worldview) of ego...which is created by ego.

CHAPTER 2

SLAVERY AND LIBERTY

The matter of free will has been discussed by all philosophers without a unanimous conclusion. Even the greatest sages of India seem to contradict themselves, affirming that everything is the work of *shakti* alone (Divine energy), but proposing a personal practice that involves individual initiative.

There is a relative approach to how I may improve my own intimate freedom, and there is a radical approach. This relative approach is more delicate to understand, for we ask this question of free will from the conviction of an individualized ego—me and non-me—which is a form of the fundamental error.

Arthur Osborne, an English disciple of Ramana Maharshi who spent ten years in his ashram when this Master was alive, and who wrote several books, used an image from the time of wireless radio when radio sets were enormous, with big tubes inside. Let's imagine that an indigenous person from an isolated tribe in the virgin forest who never had the slightest notion either of electricity or of a radio set hears the voice that comes from this huge box. This person asks, "Does the woman in the box decide which songs she can sing"—in which case it is her free will—"or are the songs imposed on her?" The answer is on another plane: There is no woman in the box.

Even if you don't know much more, it is a starting point for reflection to consider that all of this questioning about free will is asked from the conviction of ego—me, all that I am, all that I am not, my past, my future, my relationships with others—and this identification with ego is an illusion we may awake from. Such is the ultimate answer.

It is true that the more we change, the more we do not see ourselves or reality around us as before. We get the conviction that everything constantly changes, and sometimes in a very profound way—me, the other, what I want, what I refuse, what is beneficial to me, what is unfavorable to me, the way I perceive the world around me, the flow of existence. From this beginning of awakening, the question of determinism or free will does not appear in the same way, but we cannot really figure out this change in advance. It comes step by step, from one discovery to another.

Of course, a sage—whatever this one be: Tibetan, Buddhist, or Hindu—will still say to you, "Today it is a little bit cold and rainy." So when I affirm that your view of reality is "completely changed," it is not that you will see the sun when it rains, or the contrary. Ramana Maharshi, a sage who was almost unanimously considered as awakened at the highest level, recognized people very well, calling them by their own names, and he could ask, "Has your son passed his exam successfully?" or "Did your daughter recover from her cold?" This very simple human aspect of Ramana Maharshi does not appear in *Talks of Bhagavan*, nor much in all that has been written about him, but many of those who lived at his side, like Arthur Osborne or his wife, have often spoken of this to me.

You probably know the famous Zen saying that before enlightenment, mountains are mountains and rivers are rivers; during enlightenment, mountains are not mountains anymore and rivers are not rivers anymore; after enlightenment, mountains are mountains and rivers are rivers. What can you understand from this statement if you have not experienced "enlightenment," which this saying is about? Yet you feel it means something. *Oneness is not uniformity,* and consciousness of "one without a second" does not obliterate the difference between an eighteen-year-old woman and a seventy-year-old man, but our general view of relative reality, changing, being multiple, has been radically transformed. And from this transformation, the question of free will cannot be asked in the same way.

❧

What is important now is to come back to your present situation, to the question: Where is my liberty/my freedom? In relation to this theme, Gurdjieff would say, "Man is a machine set in motion by external circumstances," like a pulley making a wheel turn, and Swâmiji would talk about "a puppet, of which existence pulls the strings." Before considering immediately the ultimate view, the question of free will is asked from ego. Reading and re-reading that "ego is an illusion" does not transform you miraculously. But, in return, what becomes interesting and possible is to open yourself to this idea as expressed with the question by Gurdjieff or Swâmiji (and so many others): In what domain am I today not free, as I think I am, but a puppet or a reacting machine?

Either this assertion—that you are not free, that you are a puppet or a machine—is true or not. The truth or falsity of this becomes very concrete, as you immediately start to offer multiple observations that are part of the famous quest for self-knowledge. Whatever you want to know, you have to study it. One studies the ancient Egypt of the pharaohs' civilization; one studies molecular biology; and you may study yourself to know a little bit about who you really are. For example, you may question: What do I call "me" throughout my life? Or, Where is my margin of liberty/of freedom? And, What does my non-liberty consist of? Swâmiji would affirm, "It is the status of a slave."[1] Then you might further question: In which aspects is my status the one of a slave?

---

[1]   In English in the French text.

I have often said that one does not propose liberty/freedom as an ultimate goal to already free people. Yet the aim of the Path, of the Way—with all the efforts required for it, every step we will have to take—is Liberation. The sage in India is called *jivan mukta*, which means "liberated in this life."

To whom is "liberation" meaningful? To war prisoners in a military camp, inmates in a penitentiary or, in the past, to slaves who might be emancipated? In which aspect, and to whom or to what, am *I* enslaved? What do *I* obey? In whatever way you are enslaved, the word "liberation" would have a meaning for you. These questions, which must be considered very seriously, are obviously connected to the fundamental theme of liberty versus determinism.

Almost every person concerned with spirituality within the Eastern traditions is also touched by this word "Liberation." We are offered the possibility of such Liberation, yet we are not even clear about the forms of slavery or imprisonment that we are supposed to escape from. At the same time, however, our longing for personal freedom and wondering what our liberty or non-liberty consists of becomes at once more concrete.[2] Along with this, we may begin to question the meaning that the word "awakening" has for us, and, as a consequence, the word "sleep." I manage my life normally, I raise a family, I do my work well, we may say. Yet, in which aspects, and in which ways, does your existence continue to manifest as a "being condition," a level of consciousness, that still qualifies as a "sleeping state"?

---

[2] Here Arnaud begins to set forth the distinction, based in the teaching of Swâmi Prajnânpad, that while Liberation is the final goal, there are many pre-paratory steps on the Path, beginning with a recognition of our lack of liberty in a more internal, personal sense, particularly as regards the pull of emotions, rather than simply as freedom from external restrictions.

In the Gospels it is written, "You will know the truth and the truth will free you." (John 8:32) A Christian might only understand this as: The truth is that God is Trinitarian, so no mystic or Muslim saint who would refuse this dogma can be free.

No! The truth is the truth, that's all, and not a dogma you must stick to.

By the way, it is very interesting to notice that this word "truth," the one that will free us according to the Gospel, is translated from the Greek *alatheia*. *Lethe* means "sleep" and "oblivion," "lethargy." (Remember the river *Lethe,* the crossing of which makes souls forget their previous lives?) Whatever the mythology may be, the Greek word *lethe* implies the idea of sleep and oblivion. And the letter *a* means "without." So the word translated as "truth" etymologically implies non-sleep and non-oblivion. Jesus said to the Samaritan woman, "God is Spirit. Those who adore Him must adore Him in Spirit and in Truth" (John 4: 24), which means in non-sleep and non-oblivion. Here, for you, is a completely concrete meaning—and quite close to what a Hindu master or a Tibetan rinpoche might propose.

❧

For a long time as a young man, my practice was centered on Gurdjieff's ideas—at least those I could verify—and this verification reinforced my confidence. Gurdjieff taught that one makes nothing; everything happens. In this regard one cannot say, "I want," but "In me, that wants." I cannot say, "I speak," but "In me, it speaks." About this distinction, I later received a letter from Swâmiji, who wrote to me that the "it speaks" by Gurdjieff was "a very happy expression" as long as you do not make a "fixed and stable entity" of this "it," but merely consider it a mechanism.

Do *you* have any clue that makes you take such an affirmation seriously? And will you take seriously a teaching that speaks about

Liberation if you are not first convinced that your actions are completely mechanical and with no liberty? I freely phoned; I freely courted this woman rather than this other one. Yes—or no?

"You will know the truth and the truth will make you free" implies that, for the moment, *I* am not free. But we have an illusion of freedom: I decide, I do, sometimes I am successful, sometimes I fail, but it is *me* who acts as I want to. To see your non-liberty without doubt, you must come back to the fundamental theme, i.e., *the emotional and mental reaction that an external fact has the power to provoke in you, whether you want it or not.* About that, we have to acknowledge, it is not me who decides. If it were me, I would decide to establish myself in peace, absence of fear, serenity, joy, openness of the heart and love. I decide to be happy; and so I am. I want my heart to be completely at peace; my heart is so. I do not want to be afraid; I settle in non-fear and do not move from it.

We are obliged to recognize that the power exerted on us by the flow of existence and events that arise in the midst of the interdependence of all phenomena is the fruit of a cause-effect sequence. An event imposes an emotional reaction in you; then you worry. Another one provokes a desire; you did not decide to have such a desire, existence dictates it to you. If you never saw this dress in this shop, you would never have wanted to buy it although it is expensive. What makes one thought come into your brain rather than another thought? It is always produced from an ensemble of conditions and circumstances. How many thoughts about computers appeared in the brains of human beings during the seventeenth century? None! Inversely, how many thoughts about horse stations, oats stocks, and horseshoe makers appear in the brains of human beings today?

You do not choose the thought that comes into your brain; existence imposes it on you, in association with a certain emotional color. A fact provokes a reaction in you. The first reason why Swâmiji would say, "It is the status of a slave," was because I neither choose my desires, my emotions, nor the thoughts that come into my brain. Something makes a desire arise in *you* and not in someone else. Did you freely *not stop* in front of one shop window, and freely *stop* in front of another one? This is only a chain of causes and effects. You may believe that you do what you want, but you cannot want what you want. The most obvious fact, the least questionable statement, is that existence imposes our humors, our spirits. Today, I have no liberty. Existence commands, "Be wildly happy," and I have to be wildly happy. Existence commands, "Be desperate," and I have to be desperate. Existence commands your spirits as well as the associated state of mind, and commands the orientation of your thoughts in a certain direction. At the beginning of the Path one cannot intervene. We are identified with our reaction; we are overwhelmed, carried away by it. We cannot avoid being anxious to this degree, in spite of our desperation, so we have no liberty here—which leads some to drink, for we suffer less after the sixth pastis.[3]

One must ask the question—not in terms of free will but in terms of slavery—regarding what shows you that, at this emotional and mental level, you have no liberty: You desire but did not decide to desire. All happens by a play of action and reaction. The more we are conscious, aware, the more we observe how much—I insist purposefully—the flow of existence, of situations, of meetings, imposes changes on our inner state. Where is our real freedom at this level? Bit by bit, you will realize: I did not decide, it came like that, for I saw—or someone told me—something that touched certain predispositions in me. A word that worries me much will not disturb someone else, and inversely. One thing that will attract someone very much will not attract another one. Information that will appear to someone as very good news will seem almost meaningless to another one.

---

[3] French alcohol with anise flavor, made in Marseille, which Arnaud liked much.

You will not be *really* convinced, immediately, that your actions are not deliberate. How can I say that it is not deliberately that I decided to go see this movie rather than another one? *But a few days of honest observation are enough for you to recognize that your inner states are imposed on you.* You decide to be in a good mood, but you cannot remain in it. You decide you will not get on against your elder son, and yet you do it. You decide that something will not attract you anymore, and this desire comes back strongly. Thoughts arise in your brain without asking permission.

If a particular and precise element of self-presence and awareness does not intervene, you may come to this conclusion, which is a complete illusion: I do, I decided, I am the master, the actor, the creator of my own existence. However, lucid observation and honest reflection will lead you to bow before your non-liberty. In return, you have in you the possibility to change this situation, a possibility to undertake a walk towards Liberation that will pass through inner transformation. To know if your actions are free or not will be revealed to you little by little.

First, observe changes of your inner states: your fears, your desires, your refusals, your own mechanisms of attraction and repulsion, and where your liberty is or is not in this domain. If we do not observe ourselves, if we are not present in ourselves and to ourselves in the flow of our days, as during certain moments of interiorization in one form or another of meditation, our whole existence will only be a play of mechanical actions and reactions. With extreme awareness you will be able to approach closer to that internal liberty, which is the first step towards Liberation.

There is also a series of questions whose answers varied depending on the various schools. Namely: What makes some people enter the Path of Liberation when others are not interested in it? Is the entry done freely or is there a predisposition to it? Why do some become saints and others criminals? The doctrine proposed by Calvin, one of the founders of the Reformation with Luther, was one of predestination. In other words, one is born saved or one is born damned. Today, everyone has heard about Jesus, Buddha, or sages of India or ancient Greece. What determines why the intention to commit oneself on the Path of Liberation, or awakening, comes to someone all of a sudden?

Whether humans more or less succeed or fail at any undertaking, maintaining that they function like machines (puppets) is quite a shocking idea! This means that Napoleon was a puppet and that existence pulled "his" strings. He did not accomplish famous victories that also caused the death of many soldiers in his own army and in the enemy's ranks. This only occurred by the play of interdependence and general causality. His history is really quite prodigious: a little Corsican who becomes Emperor and who reigns for years over the whole of Europe. Was Napoleon only a reacting machine?

But it is not through mechanicality that someone becomes a saint or a sage. Forces from another level intervene. Liberation or liberty, or at least a certain degree of liberty, are obtained by our practice. Bit by bit, if a certain specific effort to enter into a more conscious and subtle relationship with this other level of reality in you is completed, you may gain a *fundamental liberty* in relation to your intimate real-life experience.

What is the mechanism that obliges you to suffer as soon as a desire that imposes itself on you cannot be completed? And how is it possible that an unavoidable and apparently scary prospect may have the power to torture you? We project on the future: In this case it will be horrible, in that case it will be wonderful. It is at the inner level of emotions, and of all the play called desire/aversion, attraction/repulsion—the great fundamental duality—that the question of freedom rests: the freedom not to be manipulated anymore by what is outside.

A piece of iron that is attracted to a magnet is not free, even though it has the illusion, Ah, I fell in love with the magnet! What? You fell in love with the magnet? No, simply, the magnet was strong and the needle stuck to it. All the play of desires is slavery. This is absolutely verifiable. A desire *imposes* itself on you (totally mechanically), and so you do not decide *freely* to desire something that you did not desire one moment before.

At first, your freedom will be freedom in relation to the emotions that the adventures in your existence have the power to raise in you; that is, those that command you to feel. You agree that you want to be free from your painful emotions, and also that you want your anxieties to disappear. But if you want to be free from torturing emotions, you must also be free from the other aspect: from happy emotions. A critic will cease hurting you only if a compliment has no power to transport you anymore. If a flattering word makes you happy, to this degree, unavoidably, a hurting word will wound you. A compliment will create in you an inner state that you did not decide to have but from which your thoughts will take a certain direction, and that will determine your reaction. If you do agree that you want to become free from your painful emotions—sadness, worry, concern, or merely annoyance and lack of ease—you must also be free from happy, temporary emotions that have nothing to do with the definitive happiness promised by spiritual teachings. Existence has to lose the power to change you inwardly like a kaleidoscope: a little shake and the image is completely modified.

Now let's take one more step connected to the theme of liberty and determinism. Try to understand the mechanism of attraction and repulsion, which manifests physically in what we call "magnetism." The piece of iron has no other possibility than being attracted to the magnet. This is slavery. Can you begin to face the theme of desires and refusals as slavery? Do you entertain the idea of being free from the mechanisms we call "attraction and repulsion" or "desire and aversion," over which you have, at first, no more liberty than the filings? You may achieve that liberty. But understand that all is connected and that, if you really want liberty, you must be free from desire as well as refusal, from attraction as well as repulsion, and you must become aware that outside conditions will no longer have the power to obligate you to desire without your having decided it.

❧

What do you recognize that you are the slave of today? There are known methods, checked through centuries, which could allow you to be really free. A change will occur in you. The sense of the individualized "me"—incomplete, frustrated—will vanish. Desires will play a less and less constraining part in your existence. To be more and more free from desire is also to be more and more free from its contraries, which are anger, fear, all forms of non-love. You will feel that egocentrism, which is our usual level of consciousness, begins to be questioned. And, bit by bit, you will perhaps come to understand this weird answer to the question, Is the woman free? Answer: There is no woman in the box.

I started by saying that we ask the question about free will from the level of ego—which means the sense of separation that engenders attraction and repulsion in relation to non-me—and not from a completely different level. We start from a statement we have to make—and which has to be confirmed—regarding our non-liberty, our slavery. We are longing for liberation...for liberty. We discover that as long as it is *me* who wants to be free, *me* who wants to be free from events, from situations, from circumstances, I am confronted with a duality: me and the other, favorable and unfavorable, reassuring or threatening. If this mechanism that reigns over our existence could be dissolved progressively, this consciousness of *me* would be dissolved in the same moment. We would perceive reality as it is, and our lacks, our frustrations, our mechanical fascinations would no longer drive us, but rather the whole situation and the appropriate answer to the whole situation would drive us instead.

What in us takes the initiative for our actions? Our desires, our refusals: I want, I don't want, I want to avoid this, I want to get that. If ego is dissolved, it is no longer me who wants or does not want. Our existence becomes a much wider participation in totality, like a musician in an orchestra who is playing the appropriate note at the appropriate moment. However, at a completely different level, we would have no other liberty except to give the right answer (which is not the egoic one) to the request of the situation. So, the astonishing formula of Swâmi Prajnânpad's: Complete slavery is perfect freedom. This is the state of internal liberty (or freedom), time after time, of the actor in a play who is completely the slave of the script and of the staging. What a relief if I may feel: Here is what has to be done, the answer to the situation. "The justice of the situation," as Swâmi Prajnânpad would say. The "will of God," as a Christian or a Muslim would say.

At the beginning of the Path, we are the slaves of our personal attractions and repulsions, of our desires and of our refusals. Along the Path, we gain some liberty. Existence does not command you anymore, Be happy! Be furious! Or at least if you *are* furious, you are not carried away by fury anymore, and you accomplish the necessary work of awareness, thanks to which fury may vanish. By practicing, changes occur in your brain circuits such that the same kinds of situations do not produce the same kinds of reactions anymore. Bit by bit, as the sense of ego diminishes, you are more and more free in relation to fears and to desires, and your actions emanate from another level in you—simple, unified, peaceful, spontaneous. From this point of view, liberty—real, ultimate liberty—is perfect harmony with the totality of reality, time after time.

This is what Hindus call, with precise meaning, "spontaneity" or "spontaneous action": evidence in the relative. In the relative, an action imposes itself on us: This is what is right to do. Right action never creates regrets, whatever the consequences may be. Existence goes on, and ego will never be the master of situations. As the *Bhagavad Gita* says: "You have the right to act, but not to the fruits of action." You always may write a letter, but there are no guarantees that the person who receives it will do what you ask her to do. A doctor is qualified and so has the right to treat his patients, but he cannot demand their healing.

The Sanskrit word *das* is translated "servant." The most beautiful is to be named Ramdas: the slave of Ram, slave of God. In dualistic or religious terms, liberation is to be the slave of God. *Abd* in Arabic also means "servant" or "slave" of one of the ninety-nine pronounceable names of God, the hundredth transcending all words. *Abd-el-Kader* means "slave of the Almighty." Liberation is to be the slave of God, and it is this kind of slave that India calls *jivan mukta*, a "living liberated person." Complete slavery is perfect freedom, beyond I want, I don't want, I was wrong, I should have, I should not have, or It does not go as I wanted. Beyond our illusion of liberty; beyond problems, frustrations, dissatisfactions, happiness which is always for tomorrow, I will be happy when..., I will be happy if..., plenitude here and now. The other shore has been reached, the trip is completed. Egocentrism is erased, and with it its world of attractions and repulsions, desires and aversions. It is this profound, intimate liberty that gets stabilized when it is no longer our fears and our desires that lead the game but our participation in the wholeness of reality, like a musician. A musician playing the *Ninth Symphony* by Ludwig van Beethoven cannot decide to play something more joyful during the whole concert: Strauss waltzes, for instance. He would only make it difficult for himself and conclude that the whole orchestra was wrong. As caricatured as this image may be, it is a good illustration of: "I don't care about what the orchestra is playing; I am not part of the whole thing." Yet, wisdom is to be part of the whole thing: "I do not especially want to play the Strauss waltzes, I want to play what is to be played." The musician may be a sublime virtuoso, yet he is enslaved to the score and to the director.

❧

Existence is not an orchestra playing under my direction a score that I have composed myself. We are included in a whole, and events go on. We may be very active, but from a permanent background of letting go. Remember Swâmi Prajnânpad's formula: "Innerly, actively passive. Externally, passively active." Dare to have a glimpse of the immense change that could occur for you. More than a change: a transformation, a metamorphosis.

About determinism and free will, we start from a form of slavery to our own conditionings such that an aspect of reality provokes in us an impulse of attraction or of repulsion, of desire or of refusal, and we gain freedom in relation to our intimate reactions and our shifts of humor. Little by little, a change that India calls "destruction of the mind" is proceeding. This wrong way of perceiving reality is always colored by our projections, and in the end we find ourselves in a certain condition that we also may represent as slavery—submission to the request of the situation I am attached to—paradoxically considered as ultimate Liberation. In fact, it is neither contradictory nor complicated. How can you be really at peace if you have to choose, to make decisions with the idea of a possible mistake? If you are, as Jean-Paul Sartre would say, "condemned to liberty." Liberation is the end of this curse.[4] The most beautiful freedom is that an appearance of choice diminishes; but, contrary to the usual slavery, the obvious gesture no longer passes through an individual ego.

Those considerations are not the interesting ideas of Swâmi Prajnânpad exposed in terms and images by Arnaud Desjardins, as one could say about the ideas of Kant, of Heidegger or Kierkegaard, about the ideas of every great Western philosopher. It is the core of the teaching you will find in every Tradition. What Swâmiji, whose ground was strict *advaita vedanta*, called "complete slavery is perfect freedom" can be heard as submission to the will of God, a God having nothing to do with the God so many times invoked throughout history to justify the worst aberrations.

You will discover bit by bit that behind these words is a reality to which we all may, if we want it, get access. There is this shore; it is slavery. The crossing is a process consisting of gaining liberty. And the other shore is another form of slavery—the only true Liberation. It is no longer slavery to the mechanicality of individual reactions by a being made of desires and fears. It is the action emanating from serene peace and love, here and now; harmony with the nature of things, which is actually slavery to truth, or to right necessity. But ego cannot know the justice of the situation, for it is blinded by its background made of frustrated desires, its background of non-reassured fears. Ordinary slavery is to ego and to the mind that makes ego incapable of understanding what its slavery is made of—a slavery

---

4   In contrast to the use of "liberty" as Arnaud has been using it throughout this chapter, meaning a step along the spiritual Path toward the ultimate Liberation, here Sartre uses the term "liberty" to refer to a fully ordinary state, or as the dictionary defines it, as a state or condition characterized by freedom from limits or restrictions.

from which it could be liberated in order to be happy at last, happy all the time.[5] Happiness...liberation...successful sadhana *is* possible, but we must change our way of seeing things and of functioning. It means actually dying at a certain level of being and consciousness in order to be reborn at a completely other level.

---

[5] For more on this, please refer to the distinction between mind and ego made in the Translator's Preface.

CHAPTER 3

THAT WHICH IS
INDESTRUCTIBLE

Having clear ideas is essential, but this does not mean that being a PhD is necessary to progress on the Path. Some people who have not studied for long have much good sense and lucidity, and some people who are supposed to be very intelligent cannot understand what their inner transformation is about.

In our usual condition—which the traditional doctrines call "sleep," "slavery," "illusion," and which all include fear—we have at our disposal a little power: our intellect. I am talking about intellect meaning a capability to see that three plus two are five; in other words, pure and impersonal intelligence. On the other hand, what matters is to understand that all the "evil" comes from the brain: from the mind and from the thoughts. The "good" will also come from the brain and from thoughts, but not from the usual functioning of the mind—this mess of cogitations distorting reality, interpreting, uselessly chewing the past, projecting with no certitude, extrapolating from a fact and drawing a wrong conclusion, completely unjustified.

Our "intellectual center" consists of two aspects. First is the "mind" that we must see objectively, with all its illusion and errors. Second, we all have, from the beginning, a certain intelligence—an intelligence that later gives access to scientific research but that already exists within the child. So it is vital to see facts lucidly, as they are. Our approach starts from here. Buddha taught much, but he also instructed to not accept anything due to the respect you have for him; think, check, find your own examples until you are convinced. In the pages ahead you will see some very unusual ideas that will not immediately be obvious to you.

What predominates in human beings is not desire, but fear. Seen from the neurological point of view, fear exists in the rough in animals. It is what makes them run when seeing a predator. It is the fear of being attacked, or the fear of dying, which all has to do with the survival instinct. But for us human beings the topic of fear becomes much more complex and, because of that complexity, much more interesting to study.

Swâmi Prajnânpad said something astonishing many times: "Fear is negative attraction." Some understand this statement at a level that is not wrong but is not the most important one, as in: If I am afraid of something I will attract it. If I'm so afraid of a car accident I will have one sooner or later because I am conditioning myself inwardly to do exactly the awkward action—not deliberately, but unconsciously—that will prove that my fear was justified. But the idea proposed by Swâmiji is different: that if we are afraid of something, in a certain way it attracts us, and yet we refuse this attraction (or this magnetism). The magnet attracts iron, not wood. Why do we have a special connection to some aspects of reality that fascinate us subtly?

One must understand well this truth of lure or attraction. There is the aspect that we recognize but resist consciously—for instance, a young priest who is sincerely committed to celibate life yet finds himself disturbed by a woman parishioner recognizes: I am attracted to her but I will not surrender to this fascination. Another simple example: I recognize that I am attracted to this grand deluxe car, but it is far outside of my financial possibilities and I won't buy it.

There are also attractions that we do not recognize that are nonetheless active. The magnet attracts iron without asking its opinion. When attraction is in play, we have the impression that it comes from us: I am intentionally interested in fancy cars; I am intentionally interested in fashion clothing by such a grand couturier. But there are attractions that play out even though we refuse them; for instance, a person who awkwardly falls from the high diving board is irresistibly, physically, attracted by gravity. But *he* does not want this attraction. He is implacably attracted and refuses to be so, like the young priest who is fascinated by a woman but is painfully divided as this attraction threatens his vocation. Some attractions have power over us and we do not agree to feel them. We do not want to recognize them, saying to ourselves, If I acknowledge this attraction, what will I become? For example, for genetic or other reasons, a father may be sexually attracted to his teenage daughter. He may agree to feel attracted to luxury cars that he cannot afford, but he will censor and repress the fact that he is attracted to his daughter. I am talking here of a father who considers himself (and is considered by others) as completely normal. This man cannot recognize his feeling; he cannot acknowledge it. The idea of incest is something too scary for him. He cannot look at it objectively. *Looking at something in an objective way obviously does not mean that we approve and become the slave of this impulse,* but we may at least try to understand, and not simply condemn, a human being who functions under the control of a sexual dynamic oriented in this direction.

You may not be personally challenged by or concerned with these particular examples, but experience shows that one is more able to understand from examples that one is *not* concerned with directly. Yet, it is important to ask yourself: Among all aspects of reality, what are those that exert an attraction on me that I refuse? We should also ask why some people have a particular fear. A woman I have known for years is scared of being tortured. Yet, those of us who live in France, in the U.S., in Switzerland, in Belgium, or in Quebec do not live in police states in which torture is an immediate and real possibility. Quite the opposite; in these countries the possibility is tiny. Why does *she* feel such a *fascination* with this topic, when in fact nobody wants to be tortured? The explanation for Swâmiji's statement is not: If I am afraid of something I will attract it; but, I am afraid *because* I am attracted to this topic or idea or person, and I refuse this attraction.

Of course, when we feel pathological physical symptoms, the idea of sickness comes to the foreground in our thoughts, at least from time to time. So we feel magnetized to the condition of a sick person—a condition that at the same time we refuse. In fact, fear will not enable us to avoid sickness, and if sickness starts, fear will not help us to overcome it. Today everybody agrees that, in addition to antibiotics and different kinds of medicines, our mental attitude has a great part to play. Dare to acknowledge: Yes, there is fear. What am I afraid of? What am I attracted to in spite of myself? Dare to admit that some magnetizations exert themselves on us and we cannot help that. We are attracted. That's it!

State the fright and then acknowledge, Yes, today I am still submitted to fear. This is the normal, ordinary, usual condition. If there are sickness symptoms, you are attracted—at the same time fearing above all the status of a sick person that might become your own. You feel this attraction and you do not agree to it, like a piece of iron that refuses to be attracted to the magnet and refuses to stick to it.

Fear is our ordinary status. Are changes in that possible? *Yes,* almost unbelievable changes, about which we have many testimonies. But do not start from the point that these changes should already have been accomplished. Fear of sickness is completely understandable. Everyone prefers to be in good condition—except for the one who might feel that sickness will be of help to his or her spiritual progress and thus be the greatest help in getting him closer to God. Fear of being tortured, as in the case of the woman I was talking of before, is more surprising. Do you see the difference? Some fears require a search in the psychological area. Why is this woman fascinated by the horror of torture, or this other person by the idea of a car accident?

What we can understand is that fear is purely an emotion—a fundamental emotion that more or less often shows up. What is the profit in fear? None! In what way does fear help you to avoid sickness? None! In what way does fear help you to avoid a car accident? None! Can you admit the very simple idea that fear, as an emotion, ruins existence *now* about a future that is *not yet here*? Above all, do you admit the idea that fear itself is a sickness you may recover from?

∂∾

It has often been said that all fears are about the fear of death. True, fear of death has been rooted within us by nature. If we had no fear of death, we would take no precaution, and that would not serve nature's interest, which is that human beings flourish on Earth. But apart from survival itself and the desire not to die now or tomorrow, the most interesting thing to observe is our fear of being destroyed. Fear of being destroyed, not fear of being killed. *Fear of being destroyed in one or another aspect of ourselves—an aspect which is actually destructible, relative, inserted in time and causality—that we are identified with.*

I may be physically destroyed by death, it is true, but the fear is not only of physical destruction. Let's take as an example a runner who has a chance to be the next Olympic champion and who has a serious accident, coming out of it badly crippled. He is still alive, but his career as a champion is over. The *man* is not dead, but the *champion* is.

The usual approach to life consists of feeling, for instance: I am lucky, I have a lot of money, I have a big fortune. To use the verb "to *have*." But the truth is, I *am* a very rich man. If this man loses his fortune because of a Stock Exchange disaster or for some other reason, his response is not, I *have* no money left. This would not hurt that much. Rather, his response would more likely be, I *am destroyed* as a rich man.

During the American depression in 1932, many "ruined" capitalists killed themselves when they lost a fortune, even though what remained of their "havings" would have seemed like a lot of money to a middle-class wage earner. Isn't it tragic? Swâmiji told me something that at first I found difficult to understand. If a mother has only one child and this child dies, it is the mother who is destroyed—*as a mother*. She cannot be a *mother* anymore. I have a child, so I am a mother, she had previously concluded. What makes a woman happy is not to *have* a child, but to *be* a mother. Yet, all these definitions (roles/labels/identifications) that we've applied to ourselves are impermanent and fragile, and this fear of them being destroyed is in the background of our existence.

In the same field of ideas, Swâmiji told me one day, "You know shooting films because you have the *being* of a cameraman." As a film director, I may say that it is true. I have been well served by the cameraman, Arnaud Desjardins, so I do understand Swâmiji. But once I got into my small room at the ashram and noted down my interview, I asked myself: Why has he said that to me? What is this formulation that mixes the verbs *to have* and *to be*? It is this: that, in fact, the *being* of a cameraman is perishable and will die if I get an eye disease and become less and less able to see well. Blindness destroys cameramen and fast car drivers, but not tenors. And it does not destroy fathers and mothers.

If a female virtuoso piano player who is also a mother loses her child, the mother is destroyed, not the piano player. One can even imagine that her suffering as a mother, if she manages to overcome it, may enrich her interpretation of some musical pieces. But an accident to her hands, even a little one, and the piano player is destroyed. She still may play a little melody to teach songs to her children, but the virtuoso has been killed. All these aspects of ourselves that we take ourselves for are destructible. While all of them will not be destroyed by aging, most of them will be. One will not have the same physical possibilities, the same memory, the same sexual magnetism.

Think about this: I have children, so is it me as a *father*, who is more or less fulfilled, disappointed, or destroyed? If my children are charming and good students, I am a happy father. If one of my sons is under the influence of a gang of young rebellious people and comes then to criminality, I am destroyed as a happy father. I *was*, and *am not* anymore.

If we replace "fear of death" with "fear of being destroyed" in regard to one or another aspect of what we are identified with, and which is changing, we can then understand that the spiritual Path is the search for what is Indestructible[1] in us: what Buddha called "Non-Born," what the Gospels call "the Kingdom of Heaven," what Vedanta calls "atman." The Path is about research into oneself: This is destructible, that is destructible. Acknowledging what is destructible is not pessimistic, but realistic. Beauty is fragile, for example. An accident to the face which plastic surgery cannot completely fix and an actress is not a star anymore. Have the courage to enquire: In what aspect of "me" am I Indestructible? Believe it or not, for some men, destruction of their hair when becoming bald is a cruel suffering. What is destroyed here? The man who had nice hair.

In spite of great victories in the medical area, a common fear today is connected to pathological clues regarding one's level of

---

[1]   Translator's note: In French, one may say, "the Indestructible," using inde-structible as a name and not only an adjective. For this reason, it is presented with a capital character here. (The title of this chapter by Arnaud is *L'Inde-structible*, The Indestructible.)

health. When, for instance, knees or shoulders hurt, it is hard; but when one's symptoms concern breathing or cardiac rhythm, it is another story. We feel ourselves threatened in our vital functions. One does not die from rheumatism in one knee, though one may die from serious cardiac weakness. If all of a sudden you feel a breathing constriction, or if your pulse becomes abnormally irregular, it is not easy to say to yourself: Fear is an emotion, and emotion is never justified. Still, however, this may become one more stimulus for you to seek what is Indestructible in yourself. You acknowledge: Yes, I may be physically destroyed by sickness and certainly I will be so some day. There is no birth without death, ever. While delivering her child the mother "gives life," and she also gives death. Consequently, it is obvious that if you feel a reasonable dread about your health, you do what has to be done—have blood tests, cardiac tests—but without thinking that you will become invulnerable, even if you put yourself on a strict diet with only self-prepared meals and take vitamins, trace elements, and Omega 3!

Today, many illusory promises try to convince us that we are going towards this indestructibility. Let's take the case of a man for whom the most important element in life was his profession: a very highly educated doctor and head of the gastroenterology unit in a big hospital. He *is* now, but when retirement comes, he *is not* anymore. The parking spot marked RESERVED FOR THE HEAD OF THE DEPARTMENT is not for him anymore, but for his successor. He is what one cruelly calls a "has-been."[2] Done.

Surely some aspects of ourselves with which we are more or less identified will not resist the flow of life. One may only estimate the degree of probability of such resistance. We are ephemeral in every aspect of ourselves and we want to deny this reality, as if such denial

---

[2]   This term was in French in the original.

was the solution. The mentality that inspires the modern world would like to make us believe that with insurance, relationships, a particular diet, we could become unalterable, invulnerable, and almighty. Neither money in the bank nor influential relationships is a guarantee.

So the question—the big one—is: Is there something, anything, of me that is immortal? True hope is not about living intelligently in order to be protected, to a certain degree, from possible destruction. That is what everyone tries to do more or less skillfully, like a famous violinist who never carried his luggage in order to avoid clenching his hands on the handles. One has to switch from the verb *to have* to the verb *to be*. Truth is not *I have a big fortune*, but *I am a rich man and I could not be so anymore*.

What remains?

Dare to face every threatened aspect of yourself! It is the only real solution. And if you really face it, you will see in yourself the unavoidable reaction, the force of which is equal and opposed: No! I will be forever young, forever rich, forever in good health.

How could that be when you will not even be the head of a unit at the hospital forever? You will be retired. And we know that, for some men—and sometimes for women—retirement is collapse. They are so psychologically destroyed that, in spite of all of their dreams of going fishing, with the psyche working on the physical body, they come to death.

All spiritual teachings dare to affirm immortality and eternal life. The most well-known prayer in the Upanishads ends with *ma amritam gamayo*—"from death lead me to immortality" (or non-death). Let's translate: From all that is destructible, lead us to what is Indestructible—call it *atman*, *Non-Born*, *Eternal Life*, *Absolute*, or *God* in you.

You may already be discovering the dawning of this realization. Perhaps the sun has not yet risen in the East, but the horizon is clearer.

The "inner sun" may not yet be ready to rise, but you feel—you have the presentiment of—its arising at some depth in yourself at another level; you have a glimpse of this "eternal present moment." And then there is no fear left. In what way could the screen be scared by the movie? No war movie can spoil the screen. Nothing can destroy this ultimate Indestructible. This testimony has been made by every sage throughout the centuries. Still, you perceive that all kinds of desires and attachments have not automatically disappeared, nor has fear of the future about some aspect of yourself that you are identified with [that you mistake yourself for[3]] disappeared.

You will have to work on your particular fear. Once you intellectually recognize that *fear changes nothing of what may happen; it is a play of the mind; it has nothing to do with here and now*, you will still not be convinced. So one must be convinced *by something positive: I want to discover what I am that is absolutely non-dependent.* What will motivate you, in every aspect of your sadhana, is this clear idea: Today, I am identified with my *relative* status. This is why human beings live in fear, as every animal does. There is no other real solution except to search for what is Indestructible by acknowledging: *Yes, this is destructible, I bow to it, I know it.* Only this perfect acknowledgement of implacable impermanence can set free the consciousness of the Eternal and dissolve the fear of death.

An intelligent dread is useful: Rain has frozen on the road; therefore, I drive with winter tires. But fear (the emotion) makes us avoid nothing, and may even encourage some totally contrary behaviors to what we pretend to want. I can only tell you that when

---

3   Translation precision in order to get closer to Arnaud's original words.

I replaced the expression "fear of death" with "fear of destruction of one aspect or another of myself that I am identified with," there was for me—simply by this change of terms—a "before" and an "after."

So let's clearly distinguish *useless fear* from *justified dread*, as in: Rain has frozen the roads; therefore, I will drive slowly or maybe not drive at all today, and go shopping some other day. Or: The weather report predicts a storm, so I will not go sailing in my small boat, as I am not a well-enough-trained skipper. But *fear*, as oppressive an emotion as it can be, is included in this "shock formula" of Swâmiji's, so often misunderstood, that "emotion is never justified." If emotion were justified it would never disappear; it would have its own reason to be. Yet, emotion *may disappear* from our existence, and it *has actually disappeared* from a sage or a saint's existence. This affirmation does not contradict the famous angers of some masters, be they Zen, Tibetan, or Sufi; Swâmi Ramdas or Mâ Anandamayî. And Swâmi Prajnânpad blessed me by expressing two incidents of anger inspired by an immense compassion. A little clarity lets us easily make the distinction between this type of anger and the usual play of reactions. This being said, however, more than thirty years spent in transmitting what I received and sharing what I understood have shown me how much the affirmation by Swâmi Prajnânpad that emotion is never justified could be misunderstood. Emotion is *never* justified, and this "never" is not to be nuanced or softened. Yet, we spend our time trying to justify emotion: It is completely normal that after what he did to me I would be angry! It cannot be otherwise. *Wrong!* You cannot today, but you can, as a human being, not be enslaved by changes of mood anymore. The human condition gives you the possibility to no longer feel ordinary emotions and to replace them with refined higher feelings. This is capital. This is the core of the Path. And this is (at first) a matter of vocabulary. What do we mean by "emotion"? What do we mean by "feeling"?

Happy *emotion* is only the contrary of painful *emotion*. *Feeling* has no contrary; it is communion with reality, whatever reality may be—the perception of reality *as it is*. Of course, the intellect has its part to play, but in order to recognize and acknowledge reality, the heart has a main role, and that's what you will discover more and more as your emotional reactions grow less. Certainly the disappearing of emotions is not itself a proof of wisdom. One day, Swâmi Prajnânpad said once again, "The sage has no emotion anymore," but then quietly added, "a brick neither." Some forms of profound mental deficiency demonstrate an absence of emotions, and some products (legal medicines or prohibited drugs) may anaesthetize them. On the other hand, the presence of emotions is the irrefutable proof that ego has not completely disappeared, that non-duality has not been reached. In this respect, based on the unanimity of all spiritual teachings in every tradition and the answers of every master I might question, let us have no doubt.

There is a kind of love that is an emotion. If the woman in your life contradicts you, you are furious, yet you pretend being much in love with her. "Love" easily changes into its contrary, but there also is a kind of love that has no contrary. If the heart participates intelligently in the perception, you may come to understand even the one who drags you to court in an unfair lawsuit. The less you have emotions, the more you see clearly. The more you see clearly in the relative, multiple, changing world, the closer you get to the world evoked by esoteric doctrines: Unity, Oneness, the Eternal, the Infinite.

This radical questioning of emotions is not only Swâmi Prajnânpad's point of view. For more than two thousand years spiritual literature—Christian literature as well as the *Bhagavad Gita* or Buddhist Scriptures—has told us again and again that the sage or the saint is settled in peace, immutable love, and equanimity; in equal humor in riches as in poverty, praise or blame, success or adversity. Think about this affirmation of Swâmiji's, but if you want to progress, do not try to soften it, to make it more flexible, or nuance it. Try to understand what emotion really is: a totally ego-centered mechanism. Ah! Yes! This is good to me. Oh! No! This is painful to me...there is *only me* in the world! Progressive disappearance of emotions is capital on the Path. It is not a little deal, but one has to be clear: I want to make it; I want to dwell in peace and love, settled in serenity and compassion.

Emotion is fundamentally useless. Apart from making us worried, confused, disturbed, or momentarily euphoric, it changes nothing, and in no case does it prepare intelligent actions. If emotions vanish, a completely different functioning of the heart will take place—one that will facilitate your possibility of perceiving reality in a totally different way. Emotion cuts us off, separates us from the wholeness we are part of. On the other hand, feeling is intelligent. It is perfectly compatible with the memory of our commitment on the Path, or the remembrance of God, or to non-identification and presence to oneself. Emotion cannot stay if at the same time you remember the practice of awareness that is proposed to you...if you remember it truly. Feeling is not threatened by self-presence; on the contrary, it gets deeper. Emotion is selfish, totally, and if you turn yourself towards the Kingdom of Heaven inside you, then a happy emotion— by which you are "beside yourself," euphoric and overexcited—loses its power.

Of course, there is an addiction to happy emotions. Unfortunately, none have ever lasted. I am beside myself in joy because... but I just heard that... and then your whole day is spoiled. Are you really convinced, first of all, that you can be free from emotions? And second, that you want to be free from emotions? Emotion has a physiological aspect (nervous, cardiac, respiratory, endocrinal) and a mental aspect: it orients thoughts in a certain direction. It cuts you off, separates you from reality, and imprisons you in a narrow world. You do not see anymore reality *as it is*. Ask yourself what you really want. Being permanently happy? Being free from fear, from suffering, from confusion, from worry, from despair? If you ruminate on a painful emotion, does it make you happy? No. What do you want: to be unhappy or happy?

One often hears that emotion is the salt of life! In order to feel emotions one watches movies, one "freaks out." This is the trap. You don't miss anything in missing emotions. You only lose the impediments to what you long for the most: the disappearance of fear, of suffering, and a very new capability to intervene—according to your possibilities—to reduce suffering within people around you. It is the contrary of selfishness. Do not engage yourself in subtleties like: There are still different types of emotions. You will see that what Swâmiji called "emotion" is very precise—one gets to see it more and more clearly—and what Swâmiji called "feeling"[4] is very precise too. This is about each and every emotion without any exception. We cannot be overexcited in joy and at the same time stand by all the suffering in the world. Emotions cut you off from yourself and from real communion with reality and others. They imprison and limit you. If you are identified with a happy emotion, you cannot be in a real relationship with anyone. You will see everything as pink. You will not be able anymore to see that your little boy looks very sad because he's been mocked at school.

Emotions are completely selfish. But what we call "feeling" is about communion—about love with no contrary. This being said, I know from experience how much this questioning of emotions may raise dread of some impoverishment and appear as a loss. Do not hear the words "to lose." Instead, hear the words "to find." You will find in yourself what is so much happier than any intensity in your

---

4   In English in the original text.

existence that emotions could bring you. Yes, there is something to lose, but the purpose is to discover, to have revealed in you, what you are truly longing for: to be at peace with yourself, relaxed, unified, with no fear, fully available for the present moment.

Overcoming of emotions and the discovery of that which is Indestructible in you are totally connected. Emotions keep you, categorically, from the revelation of the Eternal Present in you. All emotions are the play that makes us swing from fear of destruction to confronting denial of this destruction. You may be destroyed as a virtuoso piano player by an accident to your arm, but you also can be so destroyed—even if your talent remains—by the arrival on the musical scene of five or six young, very bright rivals. Then your contracts get more rare; the press does not talk of you anymore; your fame declines; and finally, though you were famous when you were twenty-five, your career is over. You know that this may happen, but is the fear unavoidable? If a world-renowned critic in an American paper wrote that you were the greatest piano player of your generation there would be a happy emotion because this would protect you from the idea that you could be destroyed as a famous virtuoso.

If, for your own sake, you go deeper into all that you have read or heard, you will see fully, clearly, the connection between what is Indestructible in you and emotions. What you lose when leaving the world of emotions is of no interest in relation to what you will discover. Existence is cheating you, fascinates you, terrifies you, causes in you all kinds of reactions, and makes you miss the essential, miss the target, the supreme aim of human existence, which is discovering the Infinite, discovering the Eternal. This is more than a change—it is a metamorphosis. And it is not minor to transform oneself. The caterpillar dies as a caterpillar to live as a butterfly, and the butterfly ascends to a new dimension. The caterpillar can only crawl. The butterfly elevates itself vertically. Metamorphosis adds a dimension that was thus far unknown.

From the ordinary point of view, this transformation is and will be baffling. We will not function anymore as we did before; we will not see things anymore as we did, but rather in a far richer way, with a comprehension of being that we did not have previously.

Changing takes time because the neuronal circuits and inertial strength of habits are well rooted in us. You will have to undertake and accomplish some skillful work to reprogram yourself. Transformation on the Path goes infinitely farther than simply not being angry in the same way. In fact, you cannot immediately gain the full understanding of what the disappearing of emotions and the stability of feeling that has no contrary—that no longer depends on circumstances—could be.

The disappearance of fear is connected to another idea which is also difficult to understand: non-separation. What does it mean to be "one with" an outer or inner phenomenon? To be "one with" and not carried away by my emotion? There are two waves in the ocean. I see them as being separated, though they are both united with the ocean. What could be your "non-separation" in regard to the policeman who arrests you on the road for exceeding the speed limit? You cannot immediately know the fullness of this experience, but you *can* feel the vibration within you of the word "communion"— that is, you can comprehend what it means to include an experience within yourself by welcoming it. You can agree that what is *is*, simply *because it is*, second by second, and you can *try* to be in communion with another person even though he is angry at you, insulting you, and appears to you as an enemy. Perhaps negativity for you pours out of him and he uses very hard, even threatening, words. Being completely in communion with him at this moment is not a usual way to function. If you achieve such communion, you will see that everything is connected. But if you still always struggle with your fears, your desires, your frustrations, your requests, with thoughts that are plaguing you, there *is* an indispensable work to do, an intimate work, and each one must do his own work, for each one is different. We do not have exactly the same fears, the same circuits carved in us that make us reactive.

There is a certain level of reality that is called "superior" or "beyond time, space, and causality" that corresponds within us to a level of consciousness and to a level of being free from all limitations. All sacred scriptures testify to it, from the Upanishads to the Gospels, as well as do some sacred art works; and one can intensely feel it in the presence of the most exceptional sages such as Mâ Anandamayî or Dilgo Khyentse Rinpoche.

Nevertheless, in order to have access to this level we need it to be represented externally by another human being who is settled in it. The sage or the spiritual master is before all the servant of this Reality. If you're watching a high-quality program on TV, you do not thank the TV set, though you owe it for seeing this program. It is not the TV set that makes the broadcast, and it is not a human being who rules this superior and deeper world which for so long has been compared to the sky in relationship to the earth. You know that the nature of the master-disciple relationship is a very important aspect of our process. The word "disciple" comes from the Latin *discipulus*, which means "student." There is the one who receives, to whom a possible path is indicated, and there is the one who transmits this teaching—who shows the way. But the "subtle" power of the sage, as great as this one can be, is limited. All of the human beings who have approached Mâ Anandamayî or stayed near Ramana Maharshi have not been transformed; have not reached peace and serenity. Let us not expect from the master something impossible.

Besides the dialogue with the disciple, the relationship with the master includes gaze exchanges, silent moments together. Some unusual influences may come to us through a human being. If you use all of what is available to you to really search in the depth—your depth—you can receive some help. *But you cannot produce anything by your own efforts, and nothing can be given to you from the outside. You can only discover what is already veiled by the usual game of desires and fears.*

Today, what is essential? It is to search for, at the very core of yourself, a level of consciousness that is free, non-dependent—that we can call, among other names, "the Immutable," "the Unalterable," "the Indestructible."[5] The work is about seeing, and seeing again clearly, that all determined aspects of our being (I am this; I am that. So am I not this; am I not that) are ephemeral. I am in good shape, so I am not sick. Inversely: I have very little money so I am poor. Thus the pure supra-individual *I Am* becomes *I am this or that*, indicating a network of limitations.

Aging may more or less affect our intellectual sharpness. Memory is alterable. And we have seen that our physical capacities may be destroyed by an accident. A pole-vaulter may find himself in a wheelchair. What *in* you is (or what *are* you that is) more profound, and which nothing can destroy? Be merely attentive to the process: what is destroyed, what is not? An athlete may be destroyed on the physical level, but when the body is paralyzed, everyone admits that consciousness is not so. Yet, we all make this mistake of taking consciousness for thoughts. If we cannot physically move anymore, we nonetheless consider that consciousness is intact. But we believe that if our thinking function did not respond anymore when required, our consciousness itself would be touched. Yet, every great spiritual tradition affirms that the *atman*, Buddha nature, or God in us is independent of our physical condition and our intellectual condition

---

[5]   All these terms are literally translated from French.

because this is about a reality from another dimension...absolute and not relative. Remember, the screen is never affected by the film. The screen here refers to definitive fullness, confidence, peace, "a peace which surpasses all human understanding," as Saint Paul (Phil. 4: 7) would say.

There comes a time when you *can* change your approach and center yourself on the Essential. The matter is no longer to acknowledge: I am less anxious; I improve the quality of my relationships; I have fewer emotions, and they do not last so long anymore. This is a very important preparatory stage. But there comes a time when you know: *Now I want what is Essential.* And this Essential is not only deeper than physical possibilities but even much deeper than thoughts. Our physical capacities may be more or less damaged, and they will be so by aging. Our intellectual function may also lessen. But if you have disengaged your heart from the mess of emotions and are settled in peace, compassion, and this kind of confidence that some describe in religious terms (for example, one feels oneself "carried in God's arms"), the function of the heart cannot be affected anymore. Nothing can reach it anymore. That's what all the sages testify. Search for what Jesus called "treasures that moth cannot devour, that rust cannot corrupt and thieves cannot steal." (Matt. 6: 19-20) This is the Core, the Heart, the deepest in yourself. Even if your physical functions deteriorate, even if your cerebral function gets less efficient, the heart function remains perfect when we have liberated it from usual emotions, which is not a small thing. We know that well.

The path to Wisdom is not a guarantee against the deterioration of the cerebral function. If this deterioration happens, two possible results may occur. The first is: I count on others. If you are immobilized, you may ask someone to bring you a glass of water. But if your memory betrays you and you ask this other one, "When did we have dinner with Mr. So-and-So?" and he replies, "Oh! I don't know!" there is a certain suffering—No! You could help me! If you don't help me I'm lost!—and this feeling feeds a useless emotion. When another betrays our expectation, we are angry with the person. And when the person you count on to help you, not physically but intellectually, does not respond to your expectation, you can see in yourself a negative reaction arising: You naughty! You don't come help me! This kind of reaction is unavoidable in human beings who have not discovered the secret of spiritual life, which would not be the case for a monk, who would have put his whole destiny into God's hands: If it's God's will that I lose my memory, I praise the Lord.

It is obvious that when your intellectual function betrays you—perhaps you go to pick up the phone, but at the very moment you want to dial you have forgotten who you wanted to talk to—one must dare the YES, the absolute YES. If you are angry with yourself, if you worry, if you add a useless refusal, you make your condition worse.

So train yourself *immediately* to the madness of the YES.

We are all concerned. A very famous dancer who had a handicapping accident is destroyed. But remember, if this man is also a great chess player, he remains intact as a chess player. Look into yourself for the Eternal, deeper than your physical feats and your intellectual achievements. The aim of the Path is not only to have fewer negative emotions and less fear; to be less and less carried away by love-affair fascinations or less upset because the stock market fell. You are not only looking for a relative freedom. Little by little, you become less and less dependent on situations and events, until metaphysical liberty is achieved. This concerns all of us. Look for this fundamental *I Am* that rust cannot destroy and that thieves cannot steal.

Search, search! Jesus promises it to you in the Gospel: "Search and you will find, knock and it will open to you." (Luke 11:9) Knock at the door of your own heart. But it will not be opened immediately. About this promise there are two parables in the Gospel. The first is about the dishonest judge. (Luke 18:1-8) An injured woman asks the judge unceasingly to dispense justice for her. Finally the judge decides to give her what she wants because he gets tired of the disturbance she creates for him every day. Jesus is very realistic. He dares to tell us to pester God, for at the end God responds to us. The other parable is the one about the sleeper who is disturbed at three in the morning by a friend asking for help, "Please, please!" (Luke 11: 5-13) The sleeper decides to get up and do his friend the favor he asks for so he can then go back peacefully to his bed and his sleep. So knock untiringly at your own heart's door. Perseverance is very clearly required from us, as it says in the Gospel.

The idea that we can be destroyed in one or another aspect of ourselves with which we are identified is capital. To switch from the verb "to have" to the verb "to be" is a great key to understanding. You may totally be able to bear that whatever you *have* may be destroyed *if* you are not affected in your *being*. For instance: I had something and I don't have it anymore. Why does this hurt me so much? I had a superb carpet and it has been stolen. I am suffering, for I am hit as the owner of this carpet. I cannot be an owner of something precious anymore!

Concerning the future, if this or that scares you, it is because there is the risk that you will be affected in one aspect of yourself that you take yourself for (identify with) today, and you know, in the background, that it is fragile. There is no guarantee of anything. If I seem to insist so much on the fact that we are not hit by what we *have* not anymore but in what we *are* not anymore, it is because of this essential idea: *The entire Path is about being; the whole Path revolves around "I Am" and the search for "Who am I?"*

Remember what Swâmiji told me one day: "You know about shooting films because you *have* the being of a cameraman." Why didn't he say, "You know about shooting films because you *are* a cameraman"? The true *I Am* is immutable. I am a cameraman, okay, but if I have an accident to my eyes? To *have* the being of a surgeon, a piano player—this is temporary. But the *atman*, the "supreme Self," the Divine, is not temporary.

So the cerebral function itself may deteriorate. But the function of the heart—peace, compassion, serenity—is indestructible when the heart is disengaged from emotions: from desires that when not achieved are cause for suffering, and from fears projected onto the future. The whole meaning of your process is to allow this Indestructible to be revealed in you; or, to say it another way, that you become settled in this absolutely non-dependent *Real*. It is this Indestructible that Buddha called, in a famous formula, the *Non-Born*: no beginning; *Non-Done*: not produced by other causes; *Non-Become*: no history, though at the surface everything unrolls in time; *Non-Composed*: though everything is composed; the brain is made of neurons and synapses, the body of cells, molecules, atoms, electrons...

Vedanta uses the expression *nitya-anitya*. *Nitya* means "eternal" but eternal does not mean thousands, millions, billions of years. Rather, it means "not involved in time," the Eternal Present. *Anitya* means "non-eternal." You will see at first only what is non-eternal. And in the expression "*atman-anatman*," *atman* is translated in English as "the Self." We may misunderstand by thinking that the expression "the Self" means "me particularly calm." No. *Atman* means *that which is existing only by itself* and not in reference to anything else. This shawl that I am wearing exists in relation to the fact that cotton fields exist too; that people cultivate them, harvest the cotton, spin it, weave it, etc. This shawl does not exist by itself. It is *anatman*.

Spiritual teachings talk about an astonishing spiritual discovery. We must ask, is it true? Or is it only a questionable idea? Generation after generation, some human beings, men and women, have affirmed that they have checked the truth of Buddha's words, or have discovered the indestructible treasures evoked by the Gospel. Therefore, you must ask: Am I nothing else than this physical body? You have recognized that your intellectual sharpness is destructible, and so you must ask: Am I nothing else than my intellectual sharpness? Even if you barely have a glimpse of what this "Non-Born" can be, you can, *right now*, have a glimpse of peace, serenity, and permanent joy, compassion, and immutable benevolence. Search for the Absolute. You will not find it at the physical level or at the intellectual level, but at the level of the heart.

Identification means mistaking yourself for something you are not really. But what you absolutely *are*, you cannot *not* be; you cannot anymore *not* be it! *I Am (aham brahmasmi, shivoham)* is eternal. Only what is added to "I Am" is perishable. Please, do not postpone this ultimate quest. The supreme aim is reserved not only for great yogis in the Himalayas or for famous mystics like Teresa of Avila and Saint John of the Cross. Do not postpone the ultimate quest.

For millenniums and in different languages, a rich and very precise vocabulary (Sanskrit, Hebrew, Arabic, old Greek, Chinese) has developed around the origin of this Ultimate Reality of being and consciousness. Due to a lack of precision in some translations, however, misunderstandings among the different traditions have arisen. Yet, when the focus is about the intimate *lived* experience of a sage or a saint, then there appears great unity—commonality—in the terms used. It is always about peace, joy, and love; about that which is a happy state independent of outer circumstances, free from oppositions of joy/sadness, peace/disturbance, love/hatred. This consistent element transcends the differences in approaches, theological or metaphysical, dualistic or non-dualistic.

What is it that, today, exiles you or tears you from infinite and immutable fullness; from that which, in truth, in the depths of your heart and in spite of surface desires and fears, you are all longing for?

CHAPTER 4

EVER PRESENT PEACE

One angle of approach to the Path is to promise us a happy state with no contrary. But why always project such a state into the future? Certainly, a sense of urgency is justified and even precious, for one's practice will thereby be more determined and intense. Yet, it is also true that wanting to go too fast is unavoidably an error. One gets out of breath, then one gives up. Skillfulness and efficacy consist of avoiding a childish rush that does not last.

Images and memories connected to a number of concerns that are shared by everyone come to our mind—such regrets, bitterness, worries are all associated with the past. Why is it that what is *not anymore* disturbs you today? I'm not saying that it should not disturb you; yes, something disturbs you, and such disturbance is very common. But these are useless thoughts. What I could have done; what I did not do; what I should have done—these are all images; representations. These are not abstract or philosophical ideas, but memories of old situations with a certain emotional coloration— "forms" that are passing one after another into you, into your spirit or your mind. One has to come back to this fundamental idea, which is Vedantic as well as tantric: *Now*—behind all these agitations that sometimes become storms of fear, despair, fury—*is the bliss of the Self*.

Many associations have taken place in us, and when a triggering factor is present, we make these same associations again, according to the same old chain of thoughts: Nobody ever understood me, nobody ever loved me; I was awkward, I was too stupid; I behaved badly, I'm guilty; I spoiled every opportunity I have had; My brother had all the chances and I had none. In fact, we are not obliged to hear all those useless inner speeches through until the end. On the contrary, as soon as possible it is important to acknowledge: These are only thoughts or images coming one after another into the field of my consciousness. *I've never been understood* is a momentary thought. The memory of a situation—associated with the context, the frame, a face—is an ensemble of images that come with an affective coloration. And in the background, here and now, the raw material of all these thoughts—that is, *Consciousness* represented by the ocean with no waves—is already present in us...and this we forget.

Yes, our existence unfolds day after day, with our successes and the domains in which we fail: with our desires that existence fulfills and those that it persists in frustrating with bad news, with trials. Those occurrences are reflected in us as emotions, thoughts, and physical feelings. Yet, the wisdom from India always insisted on this question: What happens in deep sleep? The kind of sleep that makes us say, "Oh, I slept so well." The answer is: A certain consciousness remains. If there were no consciousness anymore in some dreamless sleep, we would be afraid to fall asleep...afraid of falling into a Black Hole. While we may be scared of feeling faint—What's happening to me? My spirit is getting confused, and I'm going to fall down—still we are never afraid to go to sleep...except for children who, in their first nightmares, wake up and do not understand that they only dreamt of a tiger that does not really exist. In fact, we wish one another, "Good night, sleep tight." Sometimes one may even take a sleeping pill to fall asleep. Nonetheless, while consciousness is not fully awakened during such sleep, still there is consciousness in its pure state. During sleep we are not old or young anymore, neither man nor woman, neither famous nor unknown, neither loved nor betrayed, neither rich nor ruined. Deep sleep is always a peaceful state that attracts us—particularly if we are very unhappy. Some people who try to commit suicide by taking sleeping pills don't really want to die but to escape into the peace of sleep. If one pill makes me sleep, the whole box will provide me absolute sleep, they reason.

This peace that you contact in sleep is always here, in you, in the background, even when you are awake. Of course, there are tribulations in existence but, at this very moment, what hurts you? It is your representation of the situation, your worry about it, memories from the past, fears about the future. Yet, it is *within you* that all of this unfolds. The seeming adventure of existence unfolds between us and occurrences, between us and others' actions, between us and friends or enemies. This adventure of existence is a deal between us and the external other: my house, my wife, my children, my job, my car, my boat, my violin. But the other is also inside us: me and all the physical feelings (feelings of sickness, tensions, various pains) and the psychic feelings (fears, discouragements, despairs, anxieties) that we are in conflict with or—inversely—momentarily euphoric about. Spiritual adventure is a matter between me and me—between me as a committed disciple on the Path and what happens in my own brain, in my own heart. The good news: It is external to you. The bad news: It is external to you. But this play, this adventure, is all *in you*, in the neurons of your brain where perceptions and conceptions are following one another, including the way you interpret your own intimate feelings.

I propose for you a kind of koan from Tibetan and Japanese Buddhism. A Tibetan master asked me this famous question: A flag is flapping in the wind. What moves? The wind or the flag? Hmm... It is the flag that moves, but if there was no wind, the flag would not move. So, I imagined, the right answer would not be that the flag moves. I answered then with great assurance, "It is the wind that moves." And the master replied, "No, no! It's in your mind that it moves." This is a great answer. In the brain, something happens. The perception of a prayer flag; this is the image. The flap occurs; it is the sound. So too it is always *in you*, in the field of your consciousness, that everything manifests. All that you live unfolds in your brain, in your mind, in your psyche, in your spirit. It is only a matter of more or less precise vocabulary. In this moment, always, even in the background of some awful anguish with terrifying thoughts, a peace of depth is there: the bliss of the Self, as Hindu masters say.

Thus, in dreamless sleep we are neither *this* nor *that*, neither *not this* nor *not that*, only consciousness. But I never heard a Catholic priest or a Protestant minister announce as the theme of his sermon, "Today we're going to talk of the deep sleep," rather than commenting on some of Jesus' words from the Gospels. At first, therefore, I was surprised to acknowledge this insistence about sleep *with* dreams and sleep with *no dreams* that permeates the whole of Hindu wisdom.

☙❧

Okay! The situation *is what it is*. You don't deny it. Absolutely, you don't see the situation exactly as it is *because of your emotions*, so maybe you wrongly worry, or are wrongly glad...but still, there is a situation. And if this situation provokes worrying, painful thoughts in you, these thoughts and emotions that are so cruel appear to you as completely normal and natural, for the situation *appears to you* as cruel, threatening, hurtful. Therefore, I say it again. *Usual existence is a matter between you and the outside: friends, enemies, successes, and failures—and the Path is a matter between you and yourself.* One has to untiringly come back to this idea, for everything brings you back to consider that the game is played between you and the outside: my husband who abandoned me; my son who takes drugs; my business that goes very badly, to the point of bankruptcy...the whole range of sufferings, of which the other side of the coin would be happiness—*if* circumstances were different!

I'm not saying that the situation you feel as being "outside" is of no importance; nor that there is no value in psychotherapeutic work that allows you to change the way you enter into relationship with existential circumstances—for example, to examine why you are so convinced that you will never get access to love, or why you are sure that someone who told you something friendly cannot be sincere. Actually, you may accomplish psychological work that will improve, purify, and simplify your relationships with this "other than me." But the core of the Path is your relationship to your intimate experience, not a matter between you and the concrete situation. No! It is between you and your thoughts, *here and now*—those painful, worrying thoughts that create a chain in your brain, and thus appear to you as being completely justified and unavoidable: It's obvious that everything goes wrong outside; therefore, I'm necessarily very unhappy. It is *in you* that your existence unfolds; it is not outside. *It is in you that the cause lies, the single cause of every suffering.* And this suffering disappears during deep sleep at night. Never forget this.

We are used to identifying ourselves with mechanical changes in our inner states. But the human condition gives us the right to be at peace *now*, not only when some situation is resolved. These are two different levels of reality. Maybe your bank will actually refuse you the loan that you expect. Maybe the number of your customers and the size of your income will fall. Maybe you will have to give up your business. Yet, you have the right to serenity. You have to be able to hear that, even though all your experience tells you the contrary. If you hear that and you remember it, you have heard the most important thing.

You not only don't deny the situations that occur for you, but you welcome and assume them! A letter from your girlfriend says, "I don't want to see you anymore, I'm going with Michel and don't try to hold me back." If you put this letter under my eyes I can only say: "Yes! I do agree that these words are written for real. Your mate left you and, in addition, was aggressive towards you by writing a hurtful and humiliating letter. Yes." You can also show me the report from your accountant showing clearly that your financial situation is a disaster. And yet, I say it again: *You have a right to non-dependent peace here and now.* Yes or no, am I crazy to talk like this? What is certain is that in human history many of us have shared this craziness. Tibetan rinpoches, Hindu sages, Christian saints are equally crazy. They affirm the same truth, an expression of the same personal experience.

Be able to recognize: Here are thoughts that are coming into the field of consciousness more or less like opaque clouds in the sky, or entering onto the surface of consciousness like different kinds of waves: large, tight, tsunami-like on the surface of the ocean. The human condition does not give you the right to fly like a bird. But it does give you the right to joy, here and now, even in the worst circumstances. This is the core of the Path. Ordinary existence is a matter between you and the outer. The Path is a matter between you and the inside of you, what one cannot see from the outside. From the outside, one may see that you look sad or, contrarily, joyful. But nobody can *really* feel what you feel, or exactly know the thoughts that flow in your brain. It is not about "the situation" anymore; this is about intimate agitations and movements. A flag is flapping in the wind. What moves, the wind or the flag? It is *inside* that it moves.

If there is neither flag nor wind and you are alone in a room, with no particular decoration on the walls, what will happen? *It* will "move" in another way. Other thoughts will show up from the depth of your psyche: I did not do what I had to do; I did not live what I had to live; I did not live the true love I'm dreaming of; It's gonna be all right; I'm scared that it will turn bad... Carried away by changing states of mind, identified with chains of thoughts, you forget that in the background, at the source, there is what Buddhism calls "the true nature of spirit," completely free. Why can you not have access to it? It may require long and complex psychotherapy to lead you to a place where disturbing emotions and relationship difficulties disappear, but this practice is about remembering: *No, it's not about when I am done with my psychotherapy. It is now. I will try to recognize these thoughts merely as momentary phenomena, just like some itching, a little constipation, a headache.* In the same way that you recognize physical phenomena that come and go in you, you could observe: *Here is a certain kind of thought; here is the emotional coloration of these thoughts; here are the images that appear on the screen of consciousness. It is all on the surface; I can disengage myself from this surface, and I have a right to the underlying peace here and now.* It is always true. I do not promise that you will succeed infallibly, but dare searching in that direction.

When we are worrying, our comments can be of two sorts: What can I do to make the situation better? As in, what is necessary to improve my financial condition, or to help one of my children who is in difficulty? As a father or a mother, what can I attempt? And, on the other hand: Will I have fewer emotions if I start psychotherapy? The psychological dimension is one side of your process, that's true, and it will take time to untie what has been tied, to rectify what has been distorted, to unclog what has been clogged, like a pipe in which water cannot run anymore. But I am talking here of yet another approach, which is not incompatible. Tonight, whatever the situation may be, you will be immersed into the deep peace of dreamless sleep. Now, whatever the situation may be, you have the possibility to search for how to join with this perfect serenity while still being awake.

I remember when I was young, before Hinduism and Buddhism were in vogue, reading a book by Paul Brunton, known for his *Search in Secret India*, which revealed Ramana Maharshi to the

Western world in 1935. He also wrote *The Secret Path*, in which he talked about the tragedy of the 1914-18 War, describing bayonet fights and the use of hand grenades, mutual and absurd massacres with no decisive results between Germans and French. He wrote about front-line hospitals for the wounded before they could be evacuated. Paul Brunton quoted a doctor's report telling that after an offensive a great number of injured soldiers were regrouped in an abandoned church. We may at first figure such a situation as a hell: the moanings; the terror of the one who is frightened by having some member of his body amputated; those who were injured on the face and wondered if they would remain disfigured for the rest of their lives (the "broken faces"); men who cried out, "Kill me, it hurts too much." But the lack of sleep and exhaustion was such that at three in the morning everybody was asleep. The doctor testified, "A perfect peace reigned in the church!" From all these beings, tortured by worries and physical pains, from all these sleeping bodies, at three A.M., a total peace emanated.

Reading this book then, I didn't have the slightest glimpse of what I can testify to today. But this idea of a peace that reigned struck me in an unforgettable way. Obviously, when we wake up we find again the perception of the physical body and the world of suffering. But as we may contact this bliss when asleep, why couldn't we, whatever the context may be, contact it immediately, awake? This itself is the foundation of the practice in relation to our agitations and disturbances.

Of course, most of the time our thoughts are corresponding to a concrete situation, be it financial, social, or familial. Someone is telling you, "This is cancerous. You must have surgery to remove it." So you are tortured by worries. Yet, unanimously, spiritual teachings affirm that at this very moment *your true nature is pure consciousness*, the non-involved Infinite, the immaculate screen that serves as a background support to the movie of appearances. The "movie" is the external aspect of existence, the one a biographer may describe, the one you may talk of to others: "Guess what happened to me!" And then there is your intimate psychic history. So, for instance, two deported people may have the same outer experience. Both have a number tattooed on their arm. They are in a crowded cattle car that rolls towards Auschwitz. One of the two may be immersed in peace— this truly happened, as we have several convincing testimonies—and the other is tortured with despair, rebellious feelings, indignation, depression. If you can admit this idea, ask yourself: What would happen if, in my present situation, it was not me, but Swâmi Ramdas or Kangyur Rinpoche or another genuine sage?

At the beginning of the Path it is not about beliefs, but confidence, since every master, in every tradition, cannot have been wrong century after century. Yet they say again and again the same truth: Situations are taking place; they reflect in you as thoughts, emotions, and a certain physical feeling. The game is between you and this lived experience in the moment. And, at this very moment, already in the background of your suffering, *God is in you*. The bliss of the Self is in you, intact.

The outer situation is there, and some things probably have to be done—letters to write, actions to take—but I'm talking here of your own relationship to your own lived experience in the moment. It is here that the game is played, and here that it can be won or lost—immediately, not when you have solved your problem or fixed your financial situation. We project into the future, "when I will have purified my unconscious; when I will be done with my therapy." This is a part of the process, *but the most important is the attempt to join now this unaffected consciousness.* How are you situated in relation to your own thoughts? The more you recognize them for what they are and acknowledge that you cannot see the outer as it is because you perceive it through your emotion, the closer you get to this peace, and the more you are able to see that the external situation is less worrisome than you thought. About that, also, spiritual teachings all agree: Take care of *now;* tomorrow will take care of itself. The Gospel is clear: "Do not worry about what you will have to eat nor what you will be clothed with; even Solomon in all his splendor has not been clothed like the lilies in the fields." (Matthew 6: 25-34)

To say it simply, but plainly: *As long as you worry, you don't see clearly.* Your perception is unavoidably distorted. You only suffer from a cruel emotion and painful thoughts provoked by a situation that you do not see as it is, precisely, for it is distorted by your condemnation, by judgment or fear. In one word, by *qualification.* If you could perceive the situation with no emotion, it would not appear anymore as worrisome. And overall, you would see that the situation has no power to keep you from getting into relationship with the unaffected depth in you.

The complicated is simple. What are we longing for? To settle in serenity, joy, and the absence of fear. To stay serene in the midst of bankruptcy is more valuable than having a prosperous business but being worried. What we are looking for is already here. *We already are it.* It is the basic idea of all esoteric teaching. If you're looking for *anything* that is produced by some cause (even if that cause involves sincere efforts), the result of your searching will be possibly altered or ruined by *other* causes. What begins, ends. The Path proposes a reality to your quest that is already here, and which is not situated in time. Thoughts take place in time: Yesterday this happened; now there is that. What will happen tomorrow if it goes on this way? Yet, there is in us a Reality that is not situated in time, but in the Eternal Present. The comparison that Ramana Maharshi made with the movie screen is eloquent: The movie plays out in time; the duration of the pursuit scene is three minutes, twenty seconds. But what is the duration of the screen?

Whatever the circumstances, you may train yourself to see and recognize objectively that which is the most subjective in you. These subjectivities are often a certain type of image that do not particularly correspond to a present concrete situation. They correspond to traces from the past that are still alive in you, like stored records, which simple triggers may evoke. There is the record, "No one ever understood me." There is the record, "I never succeed; all success is for others." And there is also the record of blame and guilt. See and recognize each record, each trace from the past that you are identified with and carried away by, overwhelmed by and absorbed in.

From time to time, existence runs another and completely different record—like " Many people admire me; I always have lots of success with men (or women)." And the one of momentary optimism: "That's great, everything is going well." Some of these records we have in common with the whole of humanity; others are more personal. From the time of the world's origin, billions of joyful or desperate records have played in the brains of humans, and for twenty-five hundred years Buddhists have taught that there is actually a Non-Born, Non-Done, Non-Become, Non-Composed. It is true. If this *nirvâna* did manifest itself, directly—almost in spite of us—there would be neither Path, nor masters, nor disciples.

So one has to trust—may it be Buddha, Swâmi Prajnânpad, Mâ Anandamayî, Al-Hallaj, Jesus. *Everything goes wrong,* but you have a right to joy with no contrary.

❧

This being said, insistence on *Now* includes that you may have to deliberately change certain attitudes and habits. A memory from my youth comes to my mind. Judo had been discovered in the West shortly before WWII in 1939. In 1938, the "college of black belts" was a small, very prestigious group of adepts. At that time one could practice a kind of judo taught by the Japanese master Kawashi. Then, after the war, it was discovered that this judo was unorthodox, and that the orthodox practice was being performed in the Kodokan in Tokyo. In order to have their *dans*[1] validated by the Tokyo Kodokan, some among the early black belts had to re-train. This was after ten years or more of the training according to the Kadashi process. And they succeeded! So it is feasible to change attitudes and habits, even dramatically, but it requires patience and perseverance. You *can* re-educate yourself emotionally and mentally so that you do not function anymore in the same way. You *can* change certain neuronal circuits, certain engrams, and it will take some time. But I also want to plead a precise cause, which is that images or thoughts that disturb or anguish you are *only forms*, agitations on the surface of consciousness, or "spirit" if you prefer this term. Pay attention when you read some translated writings, for the same words do not always have the same meanings. In Buddhist literature the word "consciousness" means the whole realm of thoughts and emotions and not "Consciousness," i.e., *chit* in Sanskrit. Be clear about what you call "consciousness," "spirit," "psyche," or "mind."

There is the surface of spirit, the surface of consciousness, but peace of depth is also here, in you, unconditionally, whatever the horror of your situation may be. This depth is a reality from another level, different from all your usual experience. Remember the beautiful Sufi saying: I was roaming thirsty on the roads of the world and the jar full of water was waiting for me in my own house. All throughout Asia I found the image of the treasure hidden in the basement under the house, and of the poor creature ignoring his own wealth. But the treasure itself does not cry, "I am a treasure!" There must be someone on the outside—a Sufi or Tibetan spiritual master or a Christian mystic—to tell us all, "Search, it's already here." I also heard many times the story about the king's son who was lost as a

---

[1]   Degrees of achievement; ranks.

young child while hunting in a forest. For thirty years emissaries of his father were searching for him everywhere to give him his place back on the throne. He didn't know he was a prince, so he begged in the kingdom's streets. We all are like this prince-heir. And in "heir of the Kingdom" you probably recognize a Christian religious language. We all are heirs of the Kingdom of Heaven. These images and stories converge towards a realization that is not easy, but one that you must take into account and not forget anymore. Dare to remember them in the moment when you are lost in the thoughts and emotions that the situation seems to implacably impose on you. In that very moment, your true nature is this serenity that one could see on the faces of the wounded soldiers when immersed in peace, even if they found their nightmares arise again when waking up. (That's what the wisdom of India calls "to resorb oneself in the causal body"—the Source itself.) Why couldn't you get to it, though you already live it every night? This unconditional serenity of peaceful sleep...why couldn't you find it again when awake?

One has to train for unconditional serenity; one must try. And for that, you must be convinced that it is possible for you, and not only for a Tibetan rinpoche who did three-year retreats and then meditated for ten years alone in a cave in Sikkim or Bhutan.

What will unfold in time? Psychotherapy takes time. It takes time to correct distorted mental habits and create new connections between neurons. But you may come back again and again to this idea of *Now, what is my true, fundamental and autonomous nature?* I'm suffering; this is the surface. But the worst storms only affect the surface of the ocean.

Mind and heart may groan, *But the situation is horrible!* Leave the situation itself aside. If your house is on fire, call the firemen; but if there is no immediate necessity for action, leave the situation aside and put your attention on the way it reflects in you in the space of consciousness. *This is horrible!*—this is a thought. *But what will*

I become?—this is a thought. *Really, I don't deserve this...Why me?*—these are only thoughts. Even the cruelest emotion is momentary. It was not there eight days ago when you were so happy and joyful. Unavoidably, it will not be here anymore in two months, or even in three hours. There will be something else. It is an inner movie theater that never stops changing, a river that never stops flowing. One thought drags another, and then another. One record stops, another one starts. An inner mood fades away and another comes. But in the background *"This* that does not change" remains. Waves on the surface always change according to the direction of the wind and its ferocity, whether hard or soft; yet the ocean remains the same. *The worst cannot keep you away from being in communion with God in you. The worst can never be a reason to feel separate from God in you.* And then, you will not feel the worst as being the worst anymore, for a state of unconditional peace—of serenity, of non-worry—will arise in you. And from that state of peace, the horrible situation, the report from your accountant, or the cruel letter from your husband who has gone to live with another woman will not be seen at all with the same eyes. You do not feel them in the same way anymore. The situation is a fact, but it cannot torture you anymore. This "peace that surpasses all human understanding" is independent from situations. Then, naturally, the question becomes, What do I do? And the answer: *The whole domain of action will completely change.* You will not react anymore: write, complain, engage a trial, increase the "problems," start to drink, or even kill yourself from your inner trouble. I can promise you that what I share here is possible and real.

I remember the very moment when this change of level occurred in me. I had already tried to change emotional and mental habits, and as Swâmiji would say, "It may take time." But a day came when *here and now* imposed itself on me forever: "Like I am naked under my clothes, merely covered, in this very moment this peace is here, waiting for me in the very core of myself, the great unconditional peace whatever the situation may be and whatever my inner storm may be."[2]

Decide right now, not later on: *It is here, waiting for me, this buried treasure in my own house.* Search in yourself the Hidden Treasure. There is only one screen, but many films: a documentary about steel factories, a Western, a musical comedy, a porn film. There are countless movies. Some are of our own making, unique to us—like our favorite scenarios, enjoyable or not—and others are some that everybody has seen. And I can tell you that one of the films everybody has seen is *No One Understands Me.*

We discover, then, when seeing the same situation from this peace in the depths, that it does not appear to us as seriously as it did when we were situated at the habitual level. It is not at all scary anymore, for it has no power left to make us suffer; no power anymore to separate us from God in us, from the Infinite in us. As soon as we are captured by emotion, we do not see reality anymore. We see something threatening, so it seems only normal and unavoidable for us to be devastated by worry because the situation is so terrible. But if we find again this possible liberty, we glimpse that the situation is not that terrible. It appeared so to us because we had reacted with refusal. A whole world of worries had raised up that completely veiled our view of the whole thing. We saw only one aspect, forgetting all the rest, taking as certain some conclusions that were not at all so, not seeing the side-aspects that would have balanced our perception, nor seeing a possibility to act that would have resolved the situation, or at least made it better.

You know the common expression "lost in one's thoughts." All of this is about coming back to oneself—to self-presence—or,

---

[2]   Here Arnaud expresses his direct experience of the moment when the reality of this unconditional peace was true for him. (Translator)

according to the ascetic and mystical Christian tradition, presence to oneself and to God: I remember God. What I live *now*...I live it under God's gaze. Thus, this new element interferes with our mechanical reaction. When I remember God, with all that this word "God," "Allah," or "Ram" may represent to a mystic, I come back to myself. This is essential. It is the core of the famous Parable of the Prodigal Son. (Luke 15: 11-32) The elder son asks his father for his share of his inheritance in advance. He then goes far away, spends all of his money, and finally finds himself very unhappy in another country. He has to keep pigs, though he was born into a religion that sees pigs as unclean. And he remembers then: "In my father's house..." The story is very clear. Many authors have commented on this part. Having come back to himself, he remembered, though he had lost himself in external things.

So the first practice is to learn to come back to oneself in the midst of wandering in usual thoughts. If you are an accomplice to these thoughts, you will have no power over the torturing ones. There are all kinds of reveries—thoughts that are neither true nor useful—but at least we do not believe them too much. But when reveries become "No one understands me" or "What happens to me is unfair," we believe them.

Each time you can, wake up! You can initiate a mechanism that makes *precisely what overwhelmed or absorbed you the very thing that will trigger you to remember and thereby come back to yourself.*

There is emotion. Of that you are aware.

If you want it (and this won't happen overnight), you may create a new relationship to emotions in which their arising itself becomes the reminding factor. I'm coming back to myself and I *remember* that I am engaged on the Path. I *remember*, and all of the teaching is here, available. But if you become an accomplice to those harmless thoughts that do not torture you, you will miss an opportunity of training and maintain the mechanism of being carried away by thoughts. You reinforce that you are nothing else than your thoughts, and so, when thoughts are actually devastating because the situation appears to you as especially cruel, you will be powerless.

Train yourself. This inner freedom is in the background of the worst storms, of the greatest personal sufferings. It is also in the background of your casual, more or less happy thoughts, which are of no value compared to what is Essential—to the Infinite and the Eternal in you. If you stay at the surface of consciousness, you are wasting your time in reveries.

One can only "be" *now*. It is *here and now* that you no longer refuse what is unavoidable. You can choose, *here and now*, to no longer discuss what is not questionable. It is *now* that you yourself can put an end to the inner conflict and find again the peace that is your true nature.

CHAPTER 5

STAYING IN LOVE

In trying to say something about the "Inexpressible," Hindu doctrine uses the apophatic approach (neither this nor that) and the approach of contradictions (bigger than the biggest and smaller than the smallest; closer than the closest and farther than the farthest). But the most well-known formulation is contained in the Sanskrit word *satchitananda*, composed of *sat*, "being"; *chit*, "consciousness"; and *ananda*, "bliss."

Since my childhood I have been used to the expression "God is love," so I once told one of the most dedicated swâmis in Mâ Anandamayî's ashram about my astonishment at the fact that this term "love" does not appear in the Vedic description of the Absolute. He replied by asking me another question: "Oh! Can you conceive of bliss without love?" One word does not always go with the other, and yet, in many regards, both terms—bliss and love—are synonyms.

What meaning do we put on this word "love"?

In French,[1] it applies to very different realities, from loving God and one's fellow humans to loving milk chocolate with nuts. One may kill because of love, and this is a crime of passion. There is what each one loves; there is what each one does not love. And most of the time, when a man makes his declaration of love to a woman,

---

[1] Translator's Note: In French we only have the noun *amour* and the verb *aimer*, while in English there is at least "like" and "love." In this chapter, in order to stay close to Arnaud's words, I will only use the verb "to love" in the translation.

"I love you" actually means, "I want to be loved by you rather than by another." Love seems to be offered, but if we look at it lucidly and sincerely we'll see that this kind of love is more asked for than offered.

You must observe and understand how you function at this level. *I love what I love, and I expect something from it.* And inversely: *I don't love what I do not love.* Bit by bit, a transformation will happen. Open up to the idea of a kind of love that becomes a permanent state of being. A well-known saying is, "The sage loves like the fire heats and illuminates." Fire does not subjectively illuminate someone or something; rather, it is its nature to heat and to illuminate. One must say that this famous image is less striking to us than it was for our ancestors, for in the past there was no other way to get light than with the fire of torches and candles. And it was also only possible to get heat from the fireplace. Today, although we have both electric heaters and light, fire is so much less important to our existence, and this analogy, which we find in every traditional teaching, asks a bit more attention from us if we are to get the message from it. But the true answer to all questions about love lies in opening up to this idea: that the sage loves like the fire heats and lights. This is an unconditional love, one that does not particularly concern "someone," and yet each one may personally have a sense of this love. This love may become more and more stable, with no variations, with no contrary. Yet, look to what degree we may hate someone we once loved, for he or she has been a cause of suffering to us.

One common denominator in every spiritual teaching is that of renouncing the right we gave ourselves not to love what we do not love. If you want awakening, if you want wisdom, if you want bliss, you have to renounce not to love what you don't love, and stay settled in love independently from people or circumstances you will meet day after day. If the worst criminal gets close to a fire, it changes nothing for the fire. If someone insults the fire, speaks the harshest words that one can imagine to it, the fire continues to heat and light. In other words, the state of love implies love for enemies, love for all those we do not love. It is not that we are going to especially love someone who does not seem loveable and someone we have a tendency to criticize, but we have love for our enemies because we are settled in love. "The one who abides in love abides in God, and God abides in him," says Saint John's epistle in the New Testament. (1 John 4: 16) So the Dalai Lama abides in God, even without believing in Him.

To love does not mean to approve. *What? You're not going to ask me to love Nazis who persecuted the Jews!?*

Well, yes. The answer for every sage has always been clear: love for enemies. In a wonderful and true story, a Tibetan rinpoche who had been deported and tortured in China was liberated when Chinese politics became a bit more liberal. The Dalai Lama welcomed him and asked him, "Have you been scared sometimes?" The rinpoche replied with no hesitation, "My greatest fear has been that I would not love Chinese people anymore." To a genuine Tibetan rinpoche, that outcome would have been crueler than to be brutalized.

At the end of my first stay in a Tibetan surrounding, when shooting films in 1964-65, before going back to France I saw the Dalai Lama one last time. (We were at that time both much younger!) I asked him: "I'm going back to France to do the cutting of these films. Has Your Holiness a last instruction to give me or a request to formulate?" We were alone, just the two of us together, and he was not talking for television or newspapers. He answered, "Yes, one request: Whatever may be your love for the Tibetan people and your worship of the masters you met, never talk badly of the Chinese." And he quoted a saying of Buddha: "The fire of hatred is only extinguished by love; and if the fire of hatred does not get extinguished, it is because love was not strong enough."

The Dalai Lama had begun to talk in English with people he could trust and in situations in which his words did not apply to the future of Tibet, so in our meeting there was no interpreter. I was surprised that he used the word "love" rather than "compassion." I wondered if he understood that to Westerners the word "love"—at least at the time—was more current, more explicit, than the word "compassion."

The story of this rinpoche, whose greatest suffering was the fear that he might fail sometimes in his love for the Chinese, is a true story, like the answer of the Dalai Lama's. *Progression on the path denies us the right not to love what we consider as non-lovable.* There is no nuance at this level.

For the moment, we are far from being settled in love. We have emotional reactions of rejection, contempt, even bitterness: *I bear him a grudge.* But what is proposed here—in our own interest, not only in the interest of those we are going to love—is to stabilize ourselves bit by bit in unconditional benevolence. Yet, all of our experience since childhood is to love or not to love someone or something. I say it again: True love is a stable state of being towards which practice leads us little by little.

Then we must consider the embodiment of this love. Certainly you will spend more time and energy for your own children than for those you don't know and will never meet. You may have a special feeling for one woman or one man, for there are nuances within this state of love. In ordinary experience, when we claim to love someone and this person does not respond to our expectation—whether it is the man you're in love with or your children—the reaction is, *You make me suffer, therefore I bear you a grudge.* Children are causes of sufferings to parents, at least from time to time, and sometimes in a dramatic way. An asocial and delinquent adolescent is a heavy burden to his father and mother. The automatic response, easily understandable, is, *I do bear you a grudge, so I cannot love you anymore.*

79

It is the same reaction in an adult as in a child: *Naughty you, you hurt me!* This mechanicality is working in you, and you must decide if you want, or not, to move beyond it. The more you are settled in love, the more you are happy. One does not go without the other. They go together. All spiritual teachings promise you a happy condition—all, using different words according to different languages—one that is happy and non-dependent upon circumstances. You cannot long for this condition without clearly understanding that every non-love emotion necessarily exiles you from it. On the other hand, we all have the experience (even if it's relative, not absolute) that each time our heart is fulfilled by love, such as with our grandchildren, we are happy. Each time we are in a loving condition, we are happy.

Our usual mental functioning makes this statement: *I am kept from being happy because this person is the cause of suffering to me*, followed by, *I cannot feel love for a person who is a cause of suffering to me.* If you want the behavior of such a person to have no more power to compromise your condition of bliss, you have to see clearly and with no restriction that it is necessary that your loving condition be not affected anymore. You cannot at once be settled in this condition of bliss you are so longing for and at the same time keep a non-loving emotion in you for someone. It is impossible. The Path puts into question the usual functioning: *This I love, that I do not.* It is very simple, very clear, but totally unusual within ordinary functioning.

I will ask you a question that has to do with a cruelly traumatizing human behavior to others, to children—that of pedophilia: Do you love pedophiliacs? Your answer is probably, Of course not! But you're wrong. One has to be able to feel the same love for torturers as for victims. (I did not say that loving means approving; and I do insist on this distinction.) This is a truth that is at once one of the most clearly affirmed by all spiritual teachings and one of the most difficult to listen to. To many people the idea of having love for torturers, for "monsters," is unbearable. And yet, it cannot be otherwise. Being settled in bliss means being settled in love, and being settled in love means being settled in bliss.

Try opening to love in this way with the strong intention to succeed! Do not make of it something impossible. If your comprehension and your conviction are clear—if you can respond with love to each and every *yes but*, each objection, each doubt; if you no longer feel, That's what Buddha said, or That's what Jesus said, but instead feel, *This is my personal certitude, today. This is what I long for*—you will succeed at this settling in love much faster than you can imagine.

I insist that this is in your own interest! It is not, I have to sacrifice myself for others. Sometimes, yes, we sacrifice our selfishness for the other's happiness. (There are people who are not at all committed to a spiritual path and yet are much less selfish than some who meditate for an hour every day.) But perfect love is still beyond this kind of non-selfishness and generosity; it is an inner stable condition.

With self observation, and without immediately judging yourself, you will begin to see all that compromises this condition of perfect love. In other words, you will see every manifestation of non-love, rejection, bitterness, condemnation, and contempt. You see and recognize: *She hurt me and I bear her a grudge, but still I want to succeed in settling myself and dwelling in love.* The famous words of Jesus, "Forgive those who offended you, love your enemies, pray for those who persecute you, bless those who curse you," (Luke 6: 28) remind us of, almost literally, words from Buddha. Of course, forgiveness and blessings will not keep us from trying to protect children from pedophiliacs, but always from a base of compassion.

Society today radically turns away from love for enemies. The press condemns with no pity all of what current opinion rejects, or what the reporter personally does not like. It is non-love that reigns over humanity, and the world is suffering from it—those *who* condemn as well as those who *are* condemned. But don't demand from yourself today what you cannot realistically expect. If you do, you will fail, and you will be angry with yourself; your lack of love will start from a lack of love for yourself. There is terrible non-love for oneself: *I just was totally ridiculous*, we say of ourselves, or *I have no heart.* And at this moment we hate ourselves. When I behave this way, I've become the enemy of my own proud ego. On the other hand, to be at peace is to be settled in compassion, including for our own weaknesses, our childishness, our insane thoughts. We see and recognize. We do not approve, but we remain stable in love, which is synonymous with being settled in bliss.

Look at what—today, and throughout all your days—drags you away from this condition of love and bliss and brings you back into the play of duality and oppositions. You say: I love this kind of person; I don't love that kind of person. I love this person when he or she behaves in a certain way; I don't love this person when he or she behaves in another way. See your own impediments to this stability in love. This is possible, but it requires that we re-educate some compulsive and emotionally reactive habits. Certainly, those to whom we send benevolent thoughts rather than hostilities will benefit. Without doubt, those with whom we behave inspired by love rather than anger will benefit. But at first the greatest beneficiaries will be ourselves.

Think about these old ideas and observe if some objections arise. Objections are normal, even if certain truths have been unanimously acknowledged for millenniums by wisdom teachings. Swâmiji always succeeded in convincing me by helping me to look by myself, to see by myself.

The greatest truths are common to both the Gospels and to Buddhism, especially: Forgive those who offend you; bless those who curse you. Every day we have the opportunity to apply such teachings. We are surrounded by people who are angry with us, people who are harmful to us. One may feel oneself persecuted by one's brother-in-law, one's neighbor, or even one's mate. We then come back to a basic assumption that there is a division of existence into two sides, friendly and unfriendly. We assign a smile to the "friendly side," indicating reassurance and gratification. But if the battery is dead and our alarm clock does not ring when we had to be awakened, existence then becomes frankly "unfriendly." The alarm clock betrayed me! I had to wake up at eight-fifteen. What will I become?

With every incident that occurs, ask yourself: What effect has it on me? Do I feel it as "friendly" or "unfriendly"? "Love your enemies" implies that you completely change your attitude in relation to the "unfriendly" side of existence. Always, even if the incident is not *that* bad. For example, if someone said or did something that annoys you, it's assumed to be the hostile side of existence. Since these annoyances are minor and frequent, we do not see the connection between this unpleasant aspect of our days and the great sayings contained in the Gospels or given by Buddha. Yet, these teachings are also about such common situations, and, if you cannot apply them in relatively minor circumstances, how can you expect to apply them in very serious circumstances, when the cruel side of existence shows up, maybe through a human being, and hurts you *really* badly?

Be very attentive to this absence of neutrality and to qualifications like "good news" and "bad news"; someone's behavior that pleases me and someone else's behavior, whoever it may be, that does not please me. *Everything (no matter how small) that represents the "unfriendly" side of existence, even when not breaking your heart, is "the enemy."* "The enemy" is all that I do not love in the moment: *I wish it were otherwise.* In these very moments we must not miss the opportunity to practice. You can *try* to have loving thoughts for the situation or the person who upsets you. This turnaround, this conversion, is always available.

If you bear someone a grudge, decide—and this is already a disciple's attitude—*I will try to understand his or her behavior*. Without this about-face attitude you cannot understand his or her behavior. This you must verify for yourself. You have to agree with it. You must attempt it. If not, after twenty years you will be disappointed to have not progressed enough.

Along this line, there is an exercise called *tonglen*, taught by Tibetan masters. *Tonglen* consists of inhaling a black light that represents all the suffering or all the madness of the world, to which you open yourself, and then exhaling a white light that represents the blessing, love, all the luminous side of reality. Very concretely, in the same way, can you invert your attitude in relation to what is "the enemy," what is the "unfriendly" side of existence? In a very practical way, it is exactly in this reversal that the whole game is played. Someone behaved wrongly towards you in the past, or just now behaves wrongly with you. Understand that he or she behaves badly with you because they are trying to escape from their own suffering. Granted, he or she behaves badly with you and you bear him or her a grudge, but now you also try to reverse the situation. Buddhism teaches us: *The antidote is to have the wish for all people to be happy*. This appears at first as being theoretical, and one does not see how to put it in action. And yet, you can re-educate yourself if the decision to succeed at this reversal arises in you.

Someone is doing something that bothers you...that's simply it. But the mind starts thinking: Why did he do that? Why did she say this? Oh! I really did not need that; everything is already difficult enough. Will a time ever come when there will only be favorable situations, only enjoyable news?

This time will never come! What will come is your transformation. So remember, *Because I bear this person a grudge, I am wrong. As a committed disciple on the Path, I can no longer justify myself in bearing anyone a grudge; I now know that I am wrong.*

Another example: Previously you might have said, This person is hostile to me—or he (or she) is my enemy—because even without intentionally wanting to bother or hurt you, they just acted tactlessly. Still, you might normally react, saying, Why did he make this phone call? Now I have to write to fix this misunderstanding. It is here, at this point, that you must not miss the opportunity to do this turn-about in your attitude and to remember: Love your enemies; love the unfriendly side of existence. "Love what you do not love," as Gurdjieff recommended. Love the rain the very day you wanted sunny weather. It's very simple, but one has *to remember* and *do* the right inner gesture. This gesture will have immense efficacy. You will transform yourself, and your perception of existence will be transformed, too. The word "enemy" will disappear from your vocabulary.

Find day-to-day concrete examples. At first, "Love your enemies" seems to concern only rare and particularly serious circumstances: Israelis could maybe send loving thoughts to Palestinians and Palestinians could do the same for Israelis. But you...who will *you* address loving thoughts to? Who are *your* enemies? Maybe merely those who vote in opposition to your political opinions, for this is the unfriendly side of existence for you: that some people vote for a candidate who sounds horrible to you. In fact, we have this opportunity to love our enemies all throughout our day. If you are convinced, you will do it. And immediately "the other" will be a priority in your own mind, before "me."

When someone does something that affects you, it is *you* who are affected. At the end, even if the person behaved very badly to you, it is *you* who are disturbed. Do you want to remain upset, concerned? In one word, unhappy? Yes or no? If you don't want to remain unhappy, *decide to no more give this person the power that his or her behavior has on you today.* Whatever the situation may be, even if it is grave, it is never a reason for you to be cut off from the Divine in you. If there are air drafts, this is a reason for you to get a cold. If it rains, this a reason for you to be wet. But even the worst is never a reason to suffer. These are two different levels of reality. The worst in a movie is never a reason for the screen to be spoiled. May you be convinced and remember it. In this very moment, am I in communion with perfect peace, confidence, joy, compassion in myself? No? Then I am wrong. But do not blame yourself. When I'm saying, "I am wrong," this is a happy statement, for the fact that you are unhappy depends on *you*. Here is something that should give you immense hope: The true matter is to understand well "my mistake," and then will I be free from my suffering. Only hear this in a positive way, as a key to changing.

There is the occurrence and there is the person. We may bear some person a grudge, not only his or her action. And when we bear someone a grudge, we are the first victim of our error. *I am not speaking in favor of the person you will forgive, I am speaking in favor of your own peace of heart.* There comes a time when your conviction may be so strong that you will not waste one second anymore on cursing this person, and so harm yourself. If you want *you, now,* to be happy, you must renounce bearing anyone a grudge. And if you can reverse the situation, the "antidote"—as the Buddhists say—is to send loving thoughts to this person, to bless him or her; it is all for your benefit. Annoyances, deceptions are our daily bread; we put ourselves at the mercy of someone who acted wrongly with us, but at the end it's we who are affected.

The main point to understand is this about-face, this conversion (in Greek, *metanoia*) of our attitude in the moment when a situation represents the unfavorable side of existence. If it is just about the rain (I bear the rain a grudge the very day I planned a great sunny picnic), this is not the same mechanism that operates towards a human being. In relation to human beings, there is this background: *He or she should not have done this.* Trying to understand the reason for the behaviors of others is important, but it is not always possible. On the other hand, if true liberty/freedom is not accessible now, neither will it be tomorrow. If I decide that I cannot reverse my attitude right now, why would it be more possible to make this conversion in one year? It is *now* that the game is played, in your own interest, in order to be free from the power you gave to others to ruin your life—or at least to spoil your day. Your only chance to be free is love for your "enemies."

But when will suffering end? It will end when you...*you*...change! The world will go on running its course, but it will lose its power to disturb you. These affirmations really seem astonishing. *But I cannot change a negative emotion towards someone into love for this person!* Yes, you can, by changing some inner circuits while being inspired by Buddha or the Gospels or Swâmi Prajnânpad's words. And if *one* situation loses its power to upset you, the Path is opened before you in order that someday no situation may disturb you interiorly anymore.

Whatever happens to you, this is never a reason to feel yourself separated from this deep inner peace, which all of what we call "spirituality" is about. *If I lose my peace, it depends on me. What can I correct?* Once again, the human condition gives us a right to this peace. But this right is always compromised by something that shows up, spoiling this peace. Find your own examples; you have some every day. If you do not miss the opportunities, you will notice immense progress, more than after fifteen years of unskilled practice. In a few weeks you will discover that you have the power to completely change your view on things. The first thought that will come to your mind will be, "Staying in love," instead of "What a jerk" or even "What a bastard!" Intellectually, you will discover that this is unquestionable; that it is your only chance to free yourself—to completely change your view on facts and to elevate yourself to another level of being.

You will be fully in communion, in non-duality, with the person who in the past would have been a cause of suffering or at least of annoyance for you. One of the keys Swâmiji gave us was: "What is his or her suffering—not mine—but his or hers?" For all gestures not inspired by love are inspired by suffering or fear.

Discover for yourself this fundamental inner gesture, so contrary to one's usual experience. Usual experience is a mechanical reaction: I am full of gratitude to those who are a cause of happy emotions for me, and I bear a grudge towards those who are for me a cause of painful emotions—whatever the nature of this emotion. With this mechanical reaction it is the outside—it is the "other"—who imposes upon you, as he pleases, your negative inner states.

You can measure the inertia-strength of your habits; you can observe how readily you give in to your own mechanicality. But is that all you want? Certainly there is a type of indulgence or complacency, but you can see that it harms you. On the other hand, the Path demands much more determination from you: true decisions and a little bit of courage. It is not the psychotherapist's or the guru's job to perform a miracle. You must recognize: *I see that I'm going down and down*; and ask yourself: *Do I want to keep on going down? No!* Well then, I decide to stop. Maybe you will not stop immediately all the time, but if you decide to stop the mechanical process, all of a sudden something will crystallize, *Enough! I quit.* There will still be moments when you are going to fail, but you will not fail for good. The decision itself is essential: *I do not want to continue on this slippery way.* I do not want to suffer anymore. Is there suffering? What happens in me? What can I change? As long as I bear the other a grudge, I suffer. And then you convert your attitude into love for your enemies. Temporary enemies certainly, but to ego it is just "the enemy." If the enemy is within you, then love this enemy, forgive your weaknesses, have compassion for yourself. Yes, the enemy is also within us.

If existence at one time makes you happy and in another moment unhappy, and fundamentally never brings you safety, peace, perfect joy, it's because in the back of your mind there is always this question: *What bad thing could happen to me?*

The future is not at all guaranteed. Your situation is frustrating. This world is a valley of tears: not happy. Even if we have joyful times, existence is fundamentally disappointing, for at the end we will all grow old, we are going to die, one cannot count on anything, and what was very precious is destroyed all of a sudden. If your suffering was really dependent on others and on outer circumstances, there would be no solution. You would never be able to oblige others to be always at your service, and for the whole world to turn as an ensemble of satellites around *you*, satisfying all your desires and never upsetting you. At this level, this is a dead-end way.

In contrast, if someone shows us that our suffering *does not* depend on the other, that it depends on *us*, an immense hope then arises. Of course, you may hear this in a wrong way—as, *This is all my fault! I am guilty.* Guilty, no. But wrong, yes. And here is your only chance of salvation! If everything is the other's fault, forget all hopes. When the suffering will not be about problems with your son anymore, it will be about your boss, with your neighbor, or merely with someone that you like but who misunderstood your purposes. Then your entire day is spoiled.

It is *within you* that you can change something, and this inner revolution will completely modify your approach to existence. It will finally allow you to contact the unaltered depth and to settle into it. But for that, one must understand this precise mechanism through practicing with life's little annoyances. In some minor and annoying situation, someone played the part of the "enemy." He stole your serene condition. What will you do in order to get your perfect peace back? You have to change your inner relationship to the person who, to you, is the cause of your ill-at-easeness, of your disappointment, or of one or another form of painful emotion. Because it is the other and his or her behavior that appears to be the cause of your suffering, you have to transform your internal, intimate relationship to him or her. This is the secret, the key, that every sage proposes to us: reversing the situation in order to find yourself again united to the Unalterable in you.

"Forgive those who have offended you" is among the most famous instructions of Jesus, clearly pointed to in the "Our Father" prayer. If I really forgive those who have offended me, right now, I reverse the situation. Immediately, I feel myself in communion with God, in a state of grace. This all depends on you. Open your umbrella. *No. I don't want to be wet but I won't open my umbrella.* Our mistake is that stupid. You do not want this person to be the cause of suffering to you, so...Do you want a radical means to work with this? Then have love for him or her. *What? This bastard? I should have love for him? Never! That's the last straw! Ah! You're kidding me!* Yet, I give you this secret, the one secret that will apply to every situation.

So clearly these emotions and thoughts are yours, are *within you.* But what happens in you *depends on* the other. You may agree that it is in you that emotion resides and that it's in you that you will intervene; but still you hold that the other harmed you. Certainly you cannot avoid taking account of the other; but to change something within yourself, you must change something in your relationship to the other. What you transform in yourself is your relational mode towards the other. Rather than being angry with him or her, you have the audacity to remember your goal and the Path towards this supreme aim. You have something to change in yourself that has to do with your relationship to the other, for now the other is implied as a seeming cause of your suffering. There is no other possibility of salvation for you than this conversion: *I open myself to the other's negativity towards me.* Maybe what the other did was not especially directed towards you, but nonetheless created a disturbance for you; for instance, by harming someone you love, or by interfering in a field of activities that depended on you.

Since early childhood we have been "reacting machines." Each and every one who claims to be on the Path agrees: It is in us that something is to be changed, transformed. But I make this distinction: that the very thing we have to transform in ourselves implies the transformation of our dual relationship with the non-me; and first of all, to the terrible "enemy," while remembering that the enemy is all that affects me daily, upsets me, hurts me, disappoints me, and spoils my existence. Do not waste one second more paddling around in your own suffering. You've got the secret, the key to get out of this suffering. It is this conversion, this forgiveness, this communion.

❧

In order to progress towards the Other Shore, it is not enough to chant praises of the word "love" and to quote the famous text of Saint Paul's that "love never fails." (1Cor.13:8) I have been touched, always and forever, by manifestations of goodness, tenderness, delicacy, and concrete help coming from sages whom I approached, whatever their traditional background. Yet, too often our process remains closed, still focused around egocentrism: *my sadhana, my practice, my "egoless-state," my supra-consciousness experiences.* To say nothing of the metaphysical point of view that denies duality and thus denies another's reality and thereby the reality that there is someone else to be helped. To a little girl who asked Swâmi Prajnânpad if he had "powers" (more or less miraculous), he replied, "Infinite love, infinite patience." With such concrete testimonies of this *absolute* love, we can engage the core of the *relative* field. In order to be efficacious, expressed love has to be enlightened by intelligence and reflection.

In French versions of the Bible, the Greek term for "skillful" is often translated in different ways: wise, sensible, prudent, circumspect. Jesus himself regrets that the "children of light" are not as skillful as the "children of this world."(Luke 16:8) Loving and concretely manifesting this love requires, in fact, much skillfulness. About that, I like quoting one of the most surprising (at first) statements from Swâmi Prajnânpad: "Love is calculation." Oh no! If there is one domain in which one must not calculate, a domain that must remain beyond all measures, it is love!...is the first reaction that shows up in us.

What did Swâmiji mean here? The matter of "calculation" is not about doing addition, subtraction, and the extracting of square roots. This is not about a romantic love, but an objective love that has to do with "seeing" and not subjectively "thinking," according to our own preferences. Let's not mistake genuine love for fascination anymore. Conscious love implies the best possible conscious management of our activities—all of them. "Love is calculation" means: What will be useful to this person I pretend to love? If I do this, what will it benefit him or her in terms of generating peace within, loosening up, and developing confidence in him- or herself? Our action is rooted in the feeling of benevolence, in wanting the other to feel good. To establish communion with him or her, this love will require us to be much more intelligent than we usually are. If your wife loves every flower but tulips and each time you forget that and offer her a bouquet of tulips, your calculation is obviously wrong.

Learn to associate intellect with feeling. From that view, "love is calculation" becomes obvious. Shocking or not, this is the truth. There is an unmethodical love: *Oh, I love my children so much!* But what "calculation" do I do in their favor? *If I do this, what will be the result of it? And if I did that, what would be the result of it?* Little by little, we bring much more clarity into our manifestations of love— the love we have for our children, for our old parents, spouse or husband, or for one we feel is a fellow human. Then, "calculating" is managing measurable quantities.

With regard to this calculation business, we have three budgets to manage. One is financial: What importance will love, opening of the heart, compassion, have in the management of my money? This is extremely simple. Some very rich Indian men (I knew some) give not ten percent but forty percent of their income to feeding the poor every month. But we also have two other limited though measurable budgets to manage: our time and our energy.

Money, time, and energy are three quantities that are not infinite. Love can be infinite, but time is not. Even a sage has no more than twenty-four hours per day. How do you count your time, your energy, and of course your money? All of this is calculation. The purpose of a spiritual teaching is not to make your existence complicated, but to simplify it. Don't hear this teaching like: Oh! If we have to calculate all the time, this is exhausting! See it rather this way: If I earn more money, I will be more able to help my children, to pay for a beautiful trip for them. Yes, but earning more money might also mean working more, getting a better paid job, being less at home, and having less time to spend with my family. What is most important to your children—time or money? One can see that children whose fathers showered them with presents—You want a motorbike? I offer it to you; You want a convertible? I buy it for you—never really felt themselves fulfilled; whereas children whose fathers did not have such possibilities but were close to them—interested in their favorite sport, listened to their music—feel themselves much more fulfilled. The realities that enrich us are not necessarily financial. We may feel ourselves richer from having read something interesting, seen something beautiful, understood something important.

The management of our three budgets includes others, and also ourselves. For example: What will I do to get what I personally want? What are your priorities in order to get the "impression nourishment" that you need today? An adult no longer needs little plastic trucks into which he can put a little bit of sand, which a child enjoys. As you do your calculation, take into account what starts to grow in you, such as goodness, compassion, benevolence: Like me, others may suffer and this is cruel, to suffer, I know it. Little by little we evolve from "only me" to "me and others," then "others and me." Spiritual life is full of the miracles that occur when we begin to give more interest to others than to ourselves.

You will see that even if you are efficacious at some calculations—if you are a certified public accountant, for instance—you may be less skillful in managing these three measurable (and not at all infinite) budgets. You might be like a very badly managed company that buys too much expensive raw material and then sells its products for too low a cost on the market. Calculate more attentively, with the love for others that starts growing in you, how to use these three resources. Yes, put more and more calculation into your love, even if "love is calculation" at first seems cold and contrary to your conception.

If these words cause some uneasiness to arise in you, it shows how much you are actually run by the calculations of ego: *What will it bring for me?* Ego cannot do anything but mechanically and compulsively calculate: *If I do that, what will I earn? If I don't, what will I miss? I want, I do not want...What will it bring me that is favorable? That is unfavorable?* Ego calculates very selfishly from morning till night. The Path starts with the clear view of our egocentrism and our selfishness.

In the past, I discovered that the words "love is calculation" hit me at the very core of "my" truth—the "truth" of ego, which is *only* calculation. Ego cannot do otherwise; it is a reaction play. It may be wrong, and often is, but it hardly listens to the lessons that existence gives it. Ego asks for, asks for, asks for: *Don't hurt me, don't hit me, flatter me.* And it keeps a false accountancy in which it writes down much more of the negative than the positive; much more of what it lacks than of what it actually has. You may become indignant, saying, *I have a pure and noble heart; love is a beautiful thing, for free, and the word "calculation" comes in spoiling love.* Still, the truth remains: You know very well that you only calculate selfishly.

Here is another calculation—a completely different one. Certainly you know that "love" includes love for oneself; that one should not become a masochist, nor think that the more you frustrate yourself, deprive yourself, torture yourself, the more you will progress on the Path. Remember that this is about clarity and realism, not idealism. But Ultimate Love may be beyond measure, as it is one of the three unlimited feelings: infinite peace, compassion, and joy. The more you feel love, the more important it is for you to acknowledge what it will bring to others—to one person in particular or to others in general. As much as you can, feel yourself standing beside all the hopes and sufferings of human beings. *All—believers and atheists, famous and unknown, Chinese and Black—are, like me, happy or unhappy, joyful or desperate, rich or poor, powerful or powerless, timorous or bold.* Opening to others with compassion is at the very core of the Path, but we calculate wrongly because our mind starts interfering. And that makes us very bad accountants. Instead, we have to estimate and anticipate in a right way.

If you decide that, regarding your compassion towards others, you want to calculate rightly based merely on your personal altruism, you will come to a dead end and remain in uncertainty. In financial matters, however, if you have a calculator, you can get a result, and if someone else checks it, he will find the same total as you. You know then that your calculation is right. But about love, what will confirm that your calculation is right? We will find doubts again: I'm not sure anymore; I made that gift to my daughter and I already need to re-calculate the deal. And what about hunger in the world? My daughter has all she needs; meanwhile, people are dying from starvation. I calculated my generosity budget wrongly.

To go beyond this dead end, there is a procedure to follow. What is it that will allow you to verify that your calculation is right? Certainly you are less frightened than before, less like children begging, "Protect me, give me safety, love me, don't reject me, don't harm me." You become more and more adult, more free, more autonomous, and so are more able to act consciously, clearly; to get out from your own little circle of interests, to take much more account of others, to become wider in your view. But still you may not be sure about your decisions; you may still hesitate.

There is only one criterion: What puts you intimately at peace, true peace, here and now? This feeling, if firm, tells you that your calculation was right. If not, thoughts may always come back: I spent more than what I had to spend...so this was a selfish expense, and I should not have done it. Or, I spent generously, but I always do this for my family's advantage, while I never spend one cent for starving people in Somalia or Sudan, nor give to charity organizations that are begging for the means to buy medicines. And then along comes this astonishing criterion that at first seems to be completely selfish, but which may be the deciding factor: *In the relative sense, am I perfectly at peace?*

With so many requests, you cannot welcome all the homeless into your apartment and feed all the hungry on this planet. Ask: Do I feel myself perfectly at peace just now? Not exactly? So then, the calculation was not absolutely right. You correct it: With one more check to a humanitarian organization you participate in helping a mother who would have seen her child die in her arms get powdered milk. You did not save the whole world, but inwardly you feel yourself reunited and at peace—the peace that every spiritual doctrine promises you.

Maybe all that is required from you today is to have some rest for two hours, to just lie down and relax. This is what will bring you peace of heart for it will make you more available to do then what you have to. Calculations of love are situated in the relative, they are interdependent, and it is impossible to state only one result for all, like in mathematics. The criterion (search and you will discover that there is no other) is peace in relation to your own management, a peace that is *possible*. Ask what is required from you. Not: What is my desire? Not even: What do I feel as being right? For once again our unconscious may arise and confuse our view. There is *no other criterion* but this perfect, intimate peace. For example, you may feel that there is still one more phone call to make to your old solitary uncle, whom you do not forget. You make this call with your whole heart, but you're still not perfectly at ease. So you write a letter to a friend who is in the hospital, and you are then completely serene. This feeling is totally realistic. Do not hear, "As long as you do not save the whole world, you will never be at peace." The matter is *your peace* from now on.

Little by little you will realize that in order to remain settled in this peace, what we usually call "unselfishness" will win against selfishness. Maybe you do have, here and now, something to do for yourself—taking account of this complex machine that you are, and which has to be skillfully treated if it is to be able to be useful to others. But your peace of heart may be perfect in the relative domain *if you no longer spend your energy in useless thoughts and emotions,* because the management of these three budgets is not only the management of your own energy in the concrete management of your day-to-day life. The true management of the energy budget, whether we use this energy for ourselves or to diminish the sufferings around us, is not, first of all, about what we spend *externally* in actions. Talking takes little energy, making a gesture takes little energy, but the energy budget issue is about the *inner* management, the struggle against the sterile waste of energy in useless emotions and thoughts: *I should...I should have...Why did he say that? It was not necessary. What did I do? I'm so stupid!* We have to save gross energy—save water when we brush our teeth, switch the lights off when we leave a room, use a car that is not too heavy on gas. But the most terrible waste of energy on the face of this planet is caused by mental ruminations and sterile thinking arising from thoughts and emotions! This is also part of the "calculation"—and you will discover that there is a very bad accountant in us.

CHAPTER 6

KAMA, EROS, AND LIBIDO

Sexual energy is a very large, serious and important topic. This force animates us all, all the time. We carry it in us from birth. It is the very movement of life. All our cerebral, nervous, blood, epithelial, etc., cells are born from the fusion of two sexual cells: one ovule and one spermatozoon. Sexual energy is the fundamental manifested energy. The whole Creation that Hindus name "Manifestation" is the expression of sexual energy. And what we human beings call "sex" or the "sexual impulse" is only one aspect of it, an innate instinct that serves nature's aims for reproduction of the human species, as it does for plants and animals. Human sexuality has to take place in the collective life environment that rules the couple partnership, family life, birth, and childhood protection. So in every society there have been rules that did not allow the totally free and spontaneous expression of the sexual dynamic: that a man and a woman are both attracted to each other and have sex. The expression of the sexual impulse is not as natural in human societies as in the animal kingdom, and you will have to take account of it the best you can. In fact, everyone's mind interferes much in this domain, as does general public opinion. So what is simple becomes complicated.

To us, men and women, each time we feel non-fulfillment or frustration and consider that we might find fullness or plenitude outside of ourselves, this is a manifestation of sexual energy. Do not limit this manifestation of sexual energy to only genital functioning, even though it is the most obvious aspect. *All attraction* is always based on sexual energy. It is interesting to acknowledge that some of Sigmund Freud's ideas, mercilessly attacked when he was alive, confirmed what old teachings, especially the Hindu teachings, very precisely described. An important part of what Freud called "libido," and what in philosophical Greek vocabulary one called "eros," is the same as what the term *kama* means, i.e., "desire"—and that applies to all desires, even if one refers it first of all to sexuality. The famous *Kama Sutra*, which includes a very explicit chapter about various possible postures in which to copulate, is in fact an extensive treatise on the general theme of union between man and woman, written in the past by a very great sage.

If we don't find our plenitude—the sense that *nothing is missing in me*—inside ourselves, we look for it outside. We seek to establish union with some form of reality, no matter which one, that we feel as being outside of ourselves. Thus we establish a relationship of duality between subject and object (no matter who or what this "outside other" may be). All relative reality is a balance of attraction and repulsion. We desire union. The one who is passionate about sailing and goes to sea whenever he can on his small yacht is animated by sexual energy. He experiences union— not with a woman but with the sea. Passion for the mountains is also a manifestation of this energy; the mountaineer needs to meet with the peaks. Fundamental sexual energy may be expressed in us in different ways—not only through physical touch and a physical union between a man and a woman, or between two men or two women in the case of homosexuality. *To be alive* is to be animated by an energy that looks to express itself through complementarity: I do not find all in myself, therefore I need the sea; therefore I need the mountain; therefore I need music; therefore I need a man or a woman. The matter is always about an impulse towards "another"—an outside element; in the duality between a subject and an object. Me, I want this woman. Me, and this mountain I want to climb. Me, and this area—Caribbean or Indian Ocean—that I want to sail into.

This energy force tries to express itself through particular activities that are personal to us. Every man is not sexually attracted in the same way to every woman, or conversely. Swâmiji, who was realistic in a way that was confusing from time to time, made me notice that when one brings a cow to a bull, one has never heard the bull say no because it only loves all white cows and thus cannot be in love with a black and white one. I can tell you that this crude realism at first baffled me. I had to situate myself in a context that could lead me to go beyond my reactions. Along the same line, one reality raised in me an immense question about Hindu weddings that are decided by both families' gurus and astrologers, who choose a spouse for a young man, and the fact that most of these marriages are successful. I've known closely a lot of married couples who hadn't had a passionate love affair previous to their marriage and yet were truly very happy couples. One Hindu friend confessed to me, "I first saw my wife on our wedding day." And Swâmiji told me—very quietly one day, when we talked once again about this topic—"And at once love comes." This is an interesting topic for reflection if we want to understand human beings—and ourselves—for what seems to be so strange to us has been and still was obvious forty years ago to a great part of India. According to the *Kama Sutra*, the idea was to avoid one's mind from interfering—to avoid falling in love in the "usual way," based on unconscious projections and surface personality and not on the profound essence; a way that results in so many dissatisfying marriages. In the past, society exerted a much stronger pressure to avoid divorces and the disintegration of the family environment. Even if the wife or the husband had a lover, one maintained a certain collective structure and a seemingly harmonious marital home for the children.

We carry in us this energy that leads us to complementarity and meeting and to a natural attraction of man to woman and of woman to man. Homosexuality is not the fundamental way of nature. Sexual energy is *here*, sovereign, and you have to acknowledge it fully, without fear, in order to feel yourself alive...intensely alive. But how will you consciously manage and direct this energy? How will you allow it to express itself, taking account of all the concrete external conditions? It is easier to fulfill a desire for union with nature— sea or mountain—*when* one wants and *as* one wants, rather than to freely indulge the carnal impulse.

The fundamental manifested energy animates us and may take the specific form, one among others, of the attraction, here and now, of a man towards a woman and of a woman towards a man. To get in contact, in communion, with nature you simply have to go walking at the lakeside or into a forest...not many impediments here. But if, as a woman, you feel a very strong sexual attraction towards a man, almost at an animal level (or conversely, a man towards a woman), dare to acknowledge it. This is one aspect of your reality, not the totality of it. Suddenly feeling a strong and spontaneous physical attraction cannot be qualified as "bad," be judged and condemned. Of course, in the expression of this attraction towards another we may make mistakes that, in the end, will be causes of suffering to us and to our fellow human. But never deny—never be afraid of—the strength of life in you!

This kama impulse is normally, and most frequently, directed towards the outside. The object is a man to a woman, a mountain to a mountaineer, the sea to a sailor, a sculpture to one passionate about art. But if this impulse encounters a significant obstacle as it is directed towards the outside, it turns inward, towards oneself, and the subject then becomes object to him- or herself. This is called "self-eroticism." One has to talk about this without a judgmental attitude. The attraction that is usually directed towards another turns instead towards the inside of oneself. If the object is outside of you, you are the subject: *me*—more or less wise or more or less crazy. But the object may become yourself. It is clear in the case of a specific activity like self-eroticism (in the limited sense of that term) that judgments about the value of this activity do not change what is true. On the other hand, in a wider sense, *self-eroticism is the about-face of the life force, no longer directed towards relationship and union to another, but to oneself.* This use of sexual energy may take a non-pathological form, which is not to be condemned outright, even if it has its limitations and may be a mistake. If one's self as an ego becomes the object of one's own attraction and one's own concern, it is called "narcissism." You don't notice another woman and think she's beautiful, but instead look at yourself in the mirror and find yourself beautiful. It is not to another woman that you want to offer a fancy dress but for yourself that you are looking for the most becoming clothes. All this has to be seen clearly and dispassionately. "Seeing clearly" implies the putting aside of all *a priori* judgments. "No sense of value," Swâmiji would say. "This is right, this is wrong" will come next. If you're engaged on the Path towards wisdom, what is your direction? Towards the happiest blossoming one can wish you! How? *Without harboring any fear about your truth now.*

This impulse of interest, of attraction, turned towards oneself may take the form of a certain shutting down on oneself. Rather than investing energy in the outer world, it gets spent in reveries and fantasies. It is *me* that becomes the object of my love rather than another: man, woman, artifact, or nature.

Aside from the excessive, unbalanced forms of narcissism that are neurotic, one aspect of narcissism concerns all of us, although to different degrees. At a completely different level, this self-eroticism may also take the form of a concern for your deepest reality, the "Self" in the metaphysical sense of the term: the ocean in which you are a wave. The object of your love is no longer you as a separated and limited ego. It is *atman*, the Self, the supreme Self. Sanskrit gives us the expression *atma kama*, desire for the Self. The whole attention is turned towards the inside, towards yourself, looking for the discovery of *your* ultimate reality—the Ultimate Reality within you. This conversion is at the very core of the Upanishads and of *adhyatma yoga* (yoga towards the Self).

Start with the normal and natural fact of the impulse of life and its spontaneous expression. Look at a child at the seaside hitting the water with his or her foot for fifteen minutes just for the joy of splashing around. The activity is useless, not oriented towards any future, but he or she is happy like that. This is a game. This dynamism still animates an adult. We know that it may take perverted, sadistic, dangerous forms. But every passion is sexual—even if one says about someone else that he is "passionate about chess." It is the same word. You lived a passionate love affair with a certain woman, but you also had another passion: chess. If your passion is about more and more destructive firearms, this is also sexual, but this manifestation of the force of life leads to death.

This fundamental energy...what are you going to direct it to? Towards the Himalayan mountains, or towards bacteriological warfare? I watched on television as Madam Minister of French Defense, Minister of the Army (in the past it was men who killed one another and women who healed the wounded) proudly said that the destructive power of the French aircraft carrier ship, the *Charles de Gaulle*, was terrifying.

The force of life and interest in "something else" implies a feeling of lack, as when we are looking for love and looking to make love. These are different manifestations of the same one energy. But what is interesting is this fundamental idea—about which all contemporary psychologists would agree, even though I speak in the name of old teachings—of the primacy of the almost-always-present feeling of non-fulfillment; the subject-to-object dualistic relationship; the desire for union. As long as the mountaineer does not reach the top of the mountain, union is not perfect. But then, for the first time in history, an Englishman and a Nepalese *did* reach the very top of Mount Everest. For an instant, the feeling of fulfillment, of non-separation or non-duality, is perfect.

It may happen that this energy cannot be invested in the outer object that attracts you because of society's restraints or external conditions that prevent you from accomplishing this goal. But too often the *impression* that they prevent you is due to the play of the mind. I remember a young woman whom everyone found particularly pretty. She was convinced that she was ugly and therefore could not attract men. This kind of false certitude may start in childhood or in teenage years—during puberty, for instance, when an adolescent girl has big breasts in comparison with those of her friends.

See clearly if there is a concrete impediment in directing your energy towards the outer object, towards the other—anything from legal constraints to a lack of money. And don't forget the more or less *unconscious* psychic obstacles. If, for some objective or personal reason, you feel that your motion towards the other—whoever this one may be—is thwarted, then this energy, this fundamental desire, will turn towards yourself in two possible ways. One is what we identified earlier as self-eroticism, in which the subject him- or herself manifests love to themselves, including physically. The other is when the energy is directed towards the *atman. It is always me who becomes the center of my interest, but it's me at the deepest level—the Self beyond me.* If we go beyond the non-dualistic point of view and turn ourselves towards the mystical approach, it is sexual energy that we are investing in the passionate search for God, Ram, or Allah. A monk or a nun is happy in chastity and continence.

Actually, some human beings do turn away from the outer world—perhaps enter a cell, or do a three-year Tibetan Buddhism retreat—and direct most of their attention towards the inside. This spiritual process is either directed towards the Self, or Buddha-Nature—the one ocean of which each one is a wave—or it keeps the distinction between a subject and an object (the "other") outside: sometimes the "Whole Other," meaning God. This is the devotional Path and the true search for God. This is looking for God in ourselves. Even if the mystic feels, "I'm not interested in me, only God interests me," he or she is interested in God *within him- or herself.* If I'm only interested in God outside of me, then *my* God becomes the only *real* God. This is the notion that Allah is the true God, in which case then the Trinitarian God of Christians becomes infamous—and conversely. Then Muslims and Christians kill one another in the name of the God of love and mercy.

Is it scandalous for you to talk about sexuality, God, and Allah as being the same theme? In which direction are you going to direct this strength of life, this libido, this eros, this kama that animates you? Towards the sea? The mountain? Towards all that impassions you outside? Will you express your sexuality through Don Juanism by having lots of feminine conquests, even if each time you believe sincerely that you are "in love"? Will you invest it in an enduring monogamous union? Will you turn it momentarily towards yourself, towards self-eroticism in the relative sense of the term? Or will you direct it towards yourself in the esoteric sense, towards the Self, *atman*? (At this level it is no longer *my* deepest reality, but *the* deepest Reality in me.) Or, according to the subject-to-object (other than you) mode, towards God, Ram, Hari, Allah?

Be faithful to yourself in your reality today, and apply these truths to your own existence.

What are your circumstances today?

What are the possible emotional and mental blocks that you may need to overcome in order to achieve your desires without being their slave?

What can *you* attempt?

What I am suggesting here is precise inner work, which you can do to completely make peace with your impulses—work which will allow you to see how you manage the concrete conditions of your existence and turn them towards the Absolute. Very concretely, if you feel within yourself a manifested energy and you assume it as a sexual demand—a demand for making love that you cannot satisfy in this very moment—how will you allow this energy to express itself? By physical exercises, dancing, singing, or any activity that will allow this energy to not be repressed? Or by an ascetic practice of acceptance and transcendence? If the latter, then you are uniting yourself with the feeling of frustration.

This fundamental energy appears in the sexual-life demands that psychologists and sexologists are interested in, especially in all that concerns, facilitates, or blocks orgasm. There are three ways to use sexual energy: 1. the normal and natural way, if conditions allow it; 2. sublimation of the energy through activities that are no longer procreative, but creative; and 3. transmutation: the search for the other is turned inside, towards the inner Kingdom. Many yogis, monks, mystics have achieved this union with the depths within themselves. Psychoanalysts and psychologists believe they have discovered obvious signs of sexual repression in Teresa of Avila, and in her writings there are actually some passages that have often been quoted and that appear "too beautiful to be true" from a psychoanalytic point of view. But one may also read these passages in a completely different way. Let's not profane what is sacred, and let's not reduce what is Divine to what is human. This remarkable woman, Teresa, transmuted her energy into mystical realization and into unceasing activity to found monasteries, and her writings still inspire us today.

But also have respect for the normal and harmonious sexual life with no inhibition or frigidity. If you feel blocks, try to move past them, *and the whole Path will help you.* Learn how to transmute this energy to avoid orientation in a disastrous direction. This can occur when you try to deny something *as it is.*

If not managed and consciously used, sexual energy becomes mingled with the energy of other functions. Normally, the intellectual center functions on intellectual energy (which gets more and more purified), and the physical center functions on physical energy. You may be quite tired physically if you have been sawing wood all day, but intellectually you may be full of energy and very eager to play chess. Physical energy is one form of vital energy; intellectual energy is another. Then there is emotional energy, and lastly "sexual" energy, according to the strictest definition of the term. If this "sexual" energy in the limited sense of the word is neither transmuted into meditation nor used normally, it will be expressed through the three other centers—intellectual, physical, and emotional—in two typical ways: one is uselessness and the other is excess. On this point, Swâmiji agreed with G.I. Gurdjieff.

I remember, at the time of our first ashram, a woman who was full of vitality and who had very recently retired after a lifetime of courage and dignity. But like someone who would brag about having never smoked in their life and so having perfect lungs, she bragged about never having had a sexual relationship with a man. When a bathroom was obviously clean, she had a need to re-clean it entirely, without having been asked to. This is the useless aspect. And when she was furiously scrubbing the bathtub, one was afraid that when she was finished there would be no bathtub left. This is the excessive aspect. Overexcitement about political opinions is similar in kind. This is sexual energy that suffuses the emotional and intellectual centers. Everything becomes "monstrous," "horrifying," "scandalous." Always—uselessness and excess.

All this must not provide you with reasons to worry, be disturbed, or discouraged from doing psychological work. Truth is always your friend. From the solid ground of truth a happy future is waiting for you; for whatever your condition may be today, the Path is always open before you. Libido, eros, kama is an immense topic in which almost every aspect of our existence takes its own place. And in this ensemble is love and sexual life—the physical union of masculine and feminine—playing a sometimes concrete but most of the time symbolic role in the tantric path. This reality may be very rich, and may also lead to many sufferings. Try quietly, and always with great confidence, to consider sexual energy within this view of wholeness. Remember, great profit from progression on the Path means that your existence will be more and more simple, natural, easy, and spontaneous—little by little in every domain.

CHAPTER 7

SHOULD ONE BE AFRAID OF THE MASTER?

As misunderstood as it can be in the contemporary sociocultural context, the role of the spiritual master (guru, sheikh, rinpoche, lama, spiritual father, or sage) is fundamental: I would even say vital. Like the patient who has peritonitis or an intestinal occlusion knows that his or her only chance of salvation is in the hands of a qualified surgeon, if you are a disciple you know that you will not "get out of it all alone." The master is the channel of an influence (or of a subtler level of reality) that surpasses his or her person. He—or she—embodies what you are longing for; he or she testifies that the promises of the Path are not illusory. The spiritual master's function far surpasses that of a teacher, an instructor, or a psychotherapist, as precious and competent as these can be to their patients. In the East that I knew, and where I have been trained, whether within the Hindu, Tibetan, Zen, or Sufic environment, the veneration towards the master is immense. One did not bow before an Afghan pir, but one kissed his hand or his garment. The memory of the masters who preceded the present master, whose chain goes back to Buddha or the Prophet, remains alive and plays its part to inspire and support the candidate to wisdom.

I said that on the Path one cannot "get out of it all alone." Get out of what? Of blindness; of total non-self-awareness; of fear. In one word: of "suffering." To describe the different aspects of the spiritual sickness we may yet be healed from, the Sanskrit vocabulary—with a few slight differences according to the schools (yoga, Vedanta, tantra, etc.)—is as rich as it is precise (even if translations are often confusing) and testifies to a remarkable and well-proven assemblage of knowledge. But the adventure of gaining wisdom is not a quiet process, and the relationship with your "beloved guru," from whom the deepest part in you expects all, will go through, at least on the surface, many vicissitudes. This has always been recognized and accepted. Doubts and fears are like milestones along the disciple's road. One guesses how disturbing, even cruel, this may be to the one who expects so much from his or her guide: The fundamental idea that inspires my spiritual process is that it is him or her (the guru) who sees clearly, and me who is groping into darkness and errors (and the false view of the real). Then comes to my mind this terrifying idea: *The master is wrong and, at least on this point, I see more clearly than he does.*

What will happen then? The first risk is denial, repression. Throughout the years, many people who put emphasis on the master's grace have been eloquent about it in order to better repress their doubts about him or her. When they are too enthusiastic in pleading their cause, they may be denying their own lack of conviction, and "great disciples" are sometimes much less open to the master's grace than they may believe. There is no reason to be impressed by another's words or accounts of their experiences in meditation or to compare oneself to them. What's important to a sick person is to get healed, not to feel the way others feel. Each one has to follow his or her own path.

If you feel yourself shut down towards the master, assuming an attitude of trying to protect yourself from him, you must dare to acknowledge it. This shutting down may not involve the intellectual level, and may still allow you to listen to "interesting ideas," but the heart refuses to open. One must be able to recognize that the source

111

of this resistance is the fear that "the other"—in this case the guru—
caused to arise in us. Therefore, one must be careful not to fall into,
and stay in, the trap of "but a disciple is beyond all dread." If there
is dread, it should become a center of interest. Questions that are to
be clearly asked are: *In what respect could the master be frightening?*
What is there to be scared of about him or her? Where could he or she
lead me that could justify such a fear? What is important is not the
thoughts that will answer these questions but the feeling itself. It is
possible to welcome this fear, to listen to it, to talk with it. Swâmiji
started all my interviews with him with these simple words: "Yes,
Arnaud." I hadn't even opened my mouth before he had already said
Yes. A candidate to wisdom allows a rendezvous with his or her fear,
and listens to it rather than running away from it. Such a candidate
avoids ignoring himself as a subject by looking for the cause of his
fear only in the object: the master.

Even if this fear and this shutting down are only due to
predispositions and imprints in your unconscious, in your own
practice, at first, skillfulness means to act *as if* they are justified. This
is the starting point to clearly see into oneself. If as soon as a patient
opened his mouth the therapist stopped him, there would be no
psychotherapy at all. If, in the beginning, as soon as I started to talk
nonsense in front of Swâmiji he had interrupted me—as he could do
a few years later, saying "only thinking"—he would have paralyzed
me. In order to allow a fear to be expressed, to manifest in order to
have the conscious experience of it, one has to give it credence: as if
this fear were saying completely true words. This temporarily allows
the *value* of this fear of the master to be experienced. It also opens
the consideration that the heart cannot shut down in the face of
completely inoffensive or neutral realities, since in principle a truly
neutral object will not create any ill-at-easeness. Who would be
scared of a chair? In what way could a chair drag anyone into a place
they do not want to go? But if this chair is an exact copy of a chair

that is associated in the unconscious with a terrifying memory from childhood, it will reopen a wound that is not completely healed and produce incomprehensible discomfort. This well-known mechanism may also interfere, as we will see, in your relationship to your master.

The right method or practice consists of letting the emotion and fear "speak" rather than denying or running away from it, and you do not need a psychotherapist to hold your hand as you look at what is in you. Consider seriously the questions, *Why do I have to protect myself from my master? Where does this inner order come from that says: Above all, do not open the door of your heart?* One willingly opens one's door to a friend, but if a visitor comes with a mask on his face and a machine gun in his hand, one bolts it. Obviously, these recommendations are easier to say than to put into action. It is, at first, often impossible to dare to recognize that you have doubts about someone who is so universally admired and worshiped as the guru. Every spiritual seeker, those in monasteries as well as in ashrams, has encountered these difficulties at one time or another. Throughout many years in the past I questioned swâmis or monks who became friends of mine about it, and all of them shared with me memories of these difficult times in their own lives.

❧

This fear of the master is not without foundation. There is a Tibetan saying, "In existence, there are two dangerous places: being behind a mule or before a guru." Yes…to inveterate mental habits, to psychic conditionings, to the "prison" itself there is danger. As long as the neophyte does not feel him- or herself questioned in their ways of functioning, as long as they hope to get wisdom while fundamentally remaining as they are, there is no fear. But the Way is not like that. It is a radical transformation. Let's say it once again: Wings won't grow on the caterpillar's back; nobody ever saw a caterpillar fly. This is a metamorphosis, and many parts of the "old man" are afraid of the views of the "new man," afraid of what is yet his liberation, his awakening. When the task is listening to impassioned lectures by a Tibetan rinpoche or a Hindu swâmi, the individualized, limited, separated ego is not questioned. Nor is it when practicing controlled breathing exercises that add a certain control of energy to one's own present condition. Yet, the Path is a complete questioning of the usual way of functioning. As we all know, the acorn dies as an acorn in order to become a fifteen-meter-high oak, not a fifteen-meter-large acorn. This simple analogy demonstrates the meaning of "transformation" or "metamorphosis," which represents a true challenge to the ordinary "me." None of us has the possibility of becoming wiser at a higher level of consciousness as long as our *being* has not changed, in a revolutionary way. The newcomer on the Path doesn't know much about what this metamorphosis consists of, even when using classic examples. But most of our human propensities—which are more or less contradictory, latent tendencies composing the seeming unity of a subject—are much on their guard about this way: this "yoga towards the Self." As long as the ego is "caressed in the direction of one's hair,"[1] it's perfect. The master is sublime and infallible. But at the point where the Path becomes more *real*, our blocking, shutting down, self-protecting and questioning reactions do arise.

Those fears have to be welcomed, acknowledged, felt. And they will inform you about *yourself* much more than about your guru. Dread is a favorable sign; the approach to the guru by someone who felt no apprehension would probably be quite superficial. Very rare are those who, because of their particular personal programming, do not feel any fear and are stable in their confidence from the very first

---

[1]   Literal translation of a French expression.

day till the end of the Path. I myself have been, at some moments, on the defensive towards Swâmiji.

A certain number of women protect themselves when the master is a man for fear of falling in love with the guru; they feel both fascination and fear. Some preparatory work is needed for a woman to dare to recognize that she is attracted towards the master as a man. She might train herself to think: This one is threatening insofar as he is still seen as a man and not as a mahatma protected by his ocher robe and his long beard.

Many other kinds of fears are also part of the Path: *What will happen to me because of my association with the guru?* Or even, *What will happen to me because of some fault of the guru?* Some genuine and recognized gurus throughout history have used apparently brutal methods to make their disciples progress, putting them in critical situations in order that they have the opportunity to engage a really intense practice. But even in schools in which the master is not threatening in the ordinary sense of the word and does not use harsh methods, uneasiness will unavoidably arise sooner or later. In these circumstances it is necessary that you first be aware of your own feelings, and do not commit the mistake of thinking about your guru from your negative emotion and your disturbance. All these thoughts have to be acknowledged without denial or judgment, and the fact that they may have no foundation must be considered.

In practice, there are three types of fears of the guru. The first has to do with projections and personal predispositions (Sanskrit: *samskaras* and *vasanas*) in relation to an authority figure who has been significant during childhood. This is a well-known dynamic, but may be decisive in each particular case. If the authority figure was your father and you experienced him as excessively severe or threatening, as soon as someone else—may it be a school teacher or a spiritual master—begins to play this "role," the memory (or the image) of this father will arise, obscuring the objective perception of the person involved in the present situation. The unconscious may even project a mother on a male guru, or a father on an extraordinary sage such as Mâ Anandamayî. As an example, I will tell my personal experience.

My father had very thin lips...which also was the case for Swâmiji. When Swâmiji appeared to me as being just a little less loving and warm than usual, I saw my father in him: *Be careful, DANGER, let's stay on the defensive.* But another projection intervened as well, having to do with a big golden watch—a fob watch—that was always beside Swâmiji during my interviews with him. Well, my grandfather on my mother's side, who embodied to me absolute love, had exactly the same watch. Swâmiji said to me later that he had immediately noticed my glances towards this watch and had played with this positive element. So you must take account of this mechanism of classic projection onto an external object, or onto the "other," which you may completely miss at first.

Then there is a second and more specific type of fear. The master represents your transformation...your questioning...the letting go of many habits...a complete turning of yourself upside down—death, at a certain level, in order to live at another one. It's normal that this view encourages dread to arise about this metamorphosis—a metamorphosis that is the best thing that may happen to a human being, yet still justifies the Tibetan formula regarding the necessity to take care when around mules and gurus.

First, always the words, "I do agree." If there is fear, this feeling has to be consciously recognized and experimented with, without inner division. Fear of being surprised in a mistake is a classic fear, but the *most* interesting is the specific fear that intervenes when a candidate to wisdom "puts his or her finger in the gears."[2] At the entrance of every ashram should be hung a sign that reads: BE CAREFUL, DANGER. Danger for the mind; danger for mechanical habits; danger for the whole neurotic structure built while trying to emotionally survive. Danger for this mixture of reproaches addressed to you and pride about your overestimated skills; for all that makes this "ego"—which is the matter at hand as soon as one speaks about spirituality.

In jails there are prisoners who have only one idea—escaping— and who become the champions of escape. But there are also prisoners who are scared by the thought of their liberation. At least in jail they do not have to deal with employment and financial anguish. They have a roof over their heads; they are fed; they are protected. And they are scared to find themselves outside in a hostile world. These are approximate, as every image is, but it is true that "liberation," as prestigious as this term may be, scares as much as it fascinates. So you have to impartially look at every element of your resistance, your distrust, your rejection of the guru. Even so, this resistance is not the least difficult aspect of a relationship with the master. His or her presence itself will generate reactions in the core of the disciple, reactions that will constitute one of the strongest opportunities for practice. Not escaping from your fears, enduring despite the ending of any momentary assurance, opening yourself to the help that the master can provide: all become possible and natural. After having protected yourself (more or less) for a long time (more or less), you will at last know the absence of fear, immense gratitude, and confident love.

The last fear relative to the master is a fear that is associated with doubt—a fear that may appear only after years of practice according

---

[2]   Literal translation of a French expression.

to the master's instructions. Sooner or later a time comes when the behavior of the guru—his or her attitudes and decisions—appears to you as incomprehensible, whatever your confidence in him or her might have been. In the past I had this painful experience around Mâ Anandamayî and—to a lesser degree—around Swâmiji. It is a well-known phenomenon that is explored in detail in spiritual literature. The possibility of the Path itself is founded on the conviction that the master knows what we do not know, understands what we do not understand, sees overall what we are not able to see today. During my twenty or so years of the search and in numerous encounters with masters, I had many occasions to verify for myself how true the master's knowledge, understanding, and seeing may be; and then—sooner or later—found that circumstances came up in which this conviction was shaken. The mind and its support of emotions takes over, imposing the conviction that the guru is wrong and that, at least on our point of concern, we see more clearly than he does. The fear then becomes that he is imposing his view on us and involving us in decisions about which we are convinced he is wrong.

In truth, the misunderstanding comes from the fact that the master has a wide view of the whole of a situation at a given moment, as well as how it will unfold in time. He "gets" all the factors and dynamism involved, while you see only a part of them—maybe quite lucidly, but outside of their relationship to the whole. You take account of only the small number of parameters that you are aware of. This word "dynamism" is essential. Relative reality is always in motion; it evolves or involves. Every decision that solves a problem today will have, in the future, its consequences, beyond the precise circumstance it was about, like seeds sown in the fall that will only germinate in spring. This enlarged time-perception concerns, of course, your personal spiritual future, but also implies the whole of the present and future work of the master: the future of his or her ashram, community; the future of all those who trust him or her.

This concept is so important that I'm going to try to be a bit more explicit. With no reference to the work of Albert Einstein in modern times, ancient schools of wisdom far back in antiquity were interested in the way we live our perception of time and space and the relationship between these two measurable dimensions. Let us start with some simple statements. Why does a traveller on the TGV[3] say that Valence is two hours and ten minutes from Paris rather than expressing this distance in kilometers? In my childhood, Valence was nine hours from Paris, though perceived as being much further (and you may only guess how it would have been perceived in the 17th century). Space and time are interdependent. What is near (space) is what is quickly (time) reached, and this speed of motion varies indefinitely according to the involved conditions. If you go further into these types of reflections, which a child is capable of, they will lead you to precious personal discoveries.

For instance, if we admit the traditional idea of a "Path" (*marg* in Sanskrit, *via* in Latin) or a "crossing towards the other shore," we imply also a distance—even if it is another kind of distance than for a trip and is not expressed in kilometers or miles—and a relative time (depending on various conditions) to travel through. But in the same way that for an astronaut Valence and Paris are simultaneously visible, "the other shore," from a certain level of view, is not separated from our present level of being and is part of one whole.

Of course, the image we see of Earth from space is current, but another comparison comes to us from the ancients. Imagine a road winding around an isolated hill. You find yourself at the base of this hill, and at the same base but on the other side another person (friendly or unfriendly) is walking towards you. You do not see

---

3   Train à Grande Vitesse (very high speed train).

him yet; you are even ignorant of his existence and his movement towards you. He is, for you, the unknown future. But to an observer situated at the top of that hill, the walker and you are both part of the present. When the person who is walking towards you passes you by—after having kindly said hello or brutally harmed you— right after the first turn he becomes part of your past, while still being part of the present to the witness who is situated higher up the hill. From this higher viewpoint your future is already there *coming to you* and your past is there *going away from you*. The elevated observer has access to a fourth dimension that you completely miss. Access to this elevated view applies to the master.

Besides those relationships that are concrete and measurable by appropriate apparatuses, there also exists a subtle network of relationships within general interdependence. And with the necessary training it is possible to get a new perception of time—of the past, the present, and the future: not foreseeing as a fortune teller could do, *but having a much wider view of the deeper dynamic that animates events and situations.* It is this perception that inspires the actions of the master.

Let's come back to the painful ill-at-easeness that may disorient the disciple and which has two potential origins. One is his or her possibly latent emotional predispositions, which are rooted in the unconscious and which, despite a few primary similarities, vary according to each student. Second is the disciple's justified conception, at whatever his or her level of understanding, of some element that is limited and isolated from the fuller context. It was in reference to these critical moments in the disciple-master relationship that Swâmi Prajnânpad sent to each member of the small group of French students a photocopied letter that, among other things, made this important distinction: *If there is doubt— and doubt is but normal and natural—you have the privilege to ask and to be convinced and not to interpret.*

But it often happens that this doubt gets repressed or denied and so is not clearly felt or seen for what it is. The idea itself—to not agree anymore with the one who we expect all and everything from—appears too difficult to be clearly acknowledged. And if this doubt does succeed in expressing itself, the fear of daring to humbly and respectfully reveal to the guru a different point of view from his—given that the guru is invested by authority as the one who clearly sees and shows the truth to others—prevents the disciple from confronting the guru with confidence. This dynamic is very well known, and I myself lived through a few situations like this. But, today, memories of these moments that were at the time so hard are now deeply happy ones for me, for they are seen as steps on the path of self-knowledge and liberty.

Do not be afraid of your fears. Welcome them, feel them, but dare to question what they tell you. As a principle, it is the disciple who is wrong rather than the master.

Let us notice, at last, that among the most common survival strategies is merely the insidious avoidance of the master. I do use this word "insidious" precisely here, for the mind is unable to clearly acknowledge it. We still have this big photo of our guru, and we continue to pretend to be his or her disciple. We confirm our faith in him from far away, but a distance grows, and the genuine relationship dissolves bit by bit. We escape then the confrontation with him and we become again what Lama Denys Teundroup calls "egodidact," with no possibility that anyone can show us what is not possible to see by ourselves. There is sometimes a certain cowardice within the candidate-to-discipleship[4] that avoids the master—for

---

[4]   Swâmi Prajnânpad said once to Arnaud: "Swâmiji has no disciple, he has only candidates to discipleship," meaning that in his view the status of "discipleship" was a highly advanced stage in the sadhana.

this candidate knows very well, in their depths, that the master will show them a truth that is contrary to their blindness, and show them that they prefer their emotion and illusion. Who will win? "If your mind lives, you die. If your mind dies, you live." Because if the master is your ego's friend—the friend to this poor "me" who would so much like to be happy at last, at peace and with no fear, and who never succeeds at it but temporarily—then the master is the unsparing enemy of your only real adversary: your own "mind."[5] Or maybe I should say: The master is your always faithful ally in your own struggle against "Satan"—"the Liar and the father of the lie" according to the Gospels—that is active inside of you, and so tricky in order to maintain you under its control.

But if you become more and more conscious of the traps and snags along the Path, then your Hope is no longer in vain, and the crossing to the other shore will be achieved some day.

---

[5] In Swâmi Prajnânpad's teaching a subtle and very important distinction is to be made between ego and mind: While ego is to be respected and listened to in order to expand till the point at which it dissolves (or becomes as wide as— or one with—the Universe), the mind is defined as the "Liar," the one who, by its lies and tricks, prevents the natural expansion of ego. So this very one has to be fought with no mercy. (See more about this subtle and somewhat difficult distinction in the Translator's Preface.)

CHAPTER 8

FOR A REALISTIC PRACTICE

It has always been said, there are different paths. You may go from Paris to Rouen or from Montreal to Quebec either by one bank of the river or by the other one. There are two roads. And not only may several roads go to the same place, but also several kinds of vehicles. In the past we talked about making the trip on a donkey's, horse's, or camel's back. You are engaged on a Path that does not ask from you, from the beginning, to dedicate yourself only to the search for the Absolute. So you will have to develop an ability in relation to yourself: what Swâmiji so simply called "to be faithful to yourself as you are situated today"; more precisely, as you are situated here and now. For instance: I want to earn more money...I want to get some new professional training. Do not create useless inner conflict for yourself, such as: I should dedicate myself to the "Indestructible," rather than being invested in what is ephemeral. Yes, all of what is relative, dependent on conditions and circumstances, may be questioned by other conditions in this unceasingly changing world. This is not the eternal ultimate reality. But *your truth*, today, is that you carry within you this desire for a certain professional success. And it's the same for all in you that asks for accomplishment.

You may fulfill your desires as someone who only functions through reactions and identification with emotions, or you may consciously manage your intention by completely assuming, without philosophizing, the impermanence of things. This is your truth today. You may live it as a reacting machine, with no practice of awareness, or you may live it as a disciple: *What I undertook met an obstacle, and I use this obstacle to progress on the Path.* You see that in this attempt for an achievement some emotions arise. And you remember that if there is an emotional element, you no longer *see*, you *think*, and that all of what you think is more or less inexact, but most of the time very inexact. *Know how to remember the main instructions of this teaching while trying to achieve what is important to your heart in the relative world.*

As a start, if a demand arises in you, do you take it on? If your demand is to poison your rival by pouring a dose of arsenic in his coffee every day, do you assume this demand? Yes or no? About the intention for professional training and a better income there is no restriction to the fact of affirming: I do assume this *vasana*, this particular desire. For other desires, it is more delicate, but don't remain divided. Yes or no? If I assume it, I assume it. "If I am a devil, let me be a devil," Swâmiji would say. How many desires or intentions arise in you behind which there is a little whisper: *Oh! I should not...*If you should not, don't. *Yes, but...*and you remain in between two chairs.[1] This is disastrous to your progression. You are not free, years are passing by, some frustrations still hang around within you. If you see that this demand is not right...well, don't do it! A little bit of courage is needed here, such as: *The thought came, but I'm not obliged to follow it. This costs me.* Or, more precisely, this costs some aspects of you, even though others may have easily renounced this demand.

We are not immediately unified. And if the judgment "this is evil" was in the eyes of an authority who left you imprinted with this message during childhood, and you do it still, then do it as a disciple. This is surrendering before the truth. Your truth today is not

---

[1]   Literal translation from a French expression.

Swâmiji's or Ramdas's truth; and the truth of Arnaud at forty-four is not the truth of Arnaud at eighty-four. "Be faithful to yourself as you are situated now," whatever projects you may go for: a love affair, a professional project, or others. I assume that, being engaged on the Path towards wisdom, you would not be involved in a venture that proposes the suffering of your enemy. If you are situated as a disciple, it will change many things. You will no more be able to obey all of what goes through your mind: every caprice, each desire, all ambitions that come into your conscious field.

If you wish better income, what could the restriction be? In what way could you be the cause of suffering to someone else in pursuing this wish? Ask yourself this question. Of course, if in a coupled relationship the husband spends all of his time, all of his energy, in an activity that has nothing to do with his wife, and if she feels herself completely forgotten—abandoned—this may become a difficulty. *I see, and I take this into account.* There is a disciple's practice that is completely compatible with your decision to look for some success that, indeed, is in the domain of what is destructible: Take all of what comes every moment as a challenge, as an opportunity, and as an occasion to progress. Something makes your accomplishment easier: Recognize the happy emotion but do not let yourself be completely carried away, overwhelmed by this dependent and momentary happiness. Something thwarts your desire for your achievement: Do not let yourself be carried away by negative emotion.

I read that during the presidential campaign in the USA, before Obama's election, a reporter asked his campaign director (first in his challenge against Hillary Clinton and then against McCain), "In one sentence, what seems to be characteristic in candidate Obama?" The campaign director replied, "When all goes right, I never saw him excited by joy, but when all goes wrong, I never saw him disturbed." I'd like to know who his guru is! He is neither carried away by happy emotion in success nor carried away in negative emotion in adversity! If Obama were Swâmiji's disciple, one could say that he had the intention to engage a new professional activity as president of the United States and no longer as senator, and meanwhile that his practice was perfect.

Accomplish your relative goals within the relative; that is, within that which is destructible. Yes, the relative is impermanent: a professional success may fall apart; a great love may be broken, even by death of one or both partners in an accident. You live in this relative world. You are not mature enough today to become a nun or a swâmi to whom nothing else but the Essential has meaning: "the Only Necessary." We follow a Path that one technically calls "Path in the world of forms": I involve myself in my professional life, my trips; I play a musical instrument and I go to concerts; I fall in love; I'm interested in my children's education, *as a disciple*. Both are compatible. Do not be *now* God-oriented—only God, infinite love, Beyond, Eternal—and *then* completely overwhelmed by your activities. One has to lead both together: your ambition (a professional or love affair achievement) and your spiritual practice. Then *all* of your very concrete existence becomes the ground for your progression on the Path, of your crossing towards "the other shore."

Do not be divided between an unrealistic ideal which is untrue for you today and your present reality. In other words, when you want something, act, *but while avoiding harm to others*. And if you do harm others, have the courage to see it. Truth, only truth, all the truth. You know that some will suffer from it, but you cannot help doing it. If not, you suffocate; you betray yourself. "*Not at the cost of your very life*," Swâmiji would say. Not that you are going to actually "die," but one may destroy oneself psychologically while remaining physically alive. It is your responsibility to see, honestly and lucidly. Your own truth today is your greatest motivation for progressing. *This is my present reality, I cannot deny it*, you must affirm. "No denial in any form whatsoever," Swâmiji has noted. *I want to change...I cannot but change.* And it is by living your truth today, as a disciple, that you become more and more able to go towards what I often speak of, which is "Complete slavery is perfect freedom." Your truth today is: What has to be done? What is right?...independent of or beyond your attractions and refusals!

❦

The great truth is to remember that *if there is emotion*—and an annoyance is an emotion, even if not intense—*you no longer see clearly.* May you be convinced of this! The mind describes facts more or less precisely—or distorts them completely—but the interpretation it gives of them and the conclusions it makes are *totally wrong.* Yes or no, is there in you the slightest element of emotion? Train yourself to welcome everything, good news and bad news, in relation to your intention of accomplishment. Play fair: Take what is favorable and also take what is unfavorable, what is reassuring and also what is threatening. This is the key to transform yourself through human pursuits that do not appear at all as "spiritual," according to the official criteria of mystical life of some hermits in a cave and monks in a monastery.

What will create a genuine Path from an ordinary existence? Whether you renounce everything and take on nothing—neither money nor a love affair, success nor power (like *sannyasins*, monks, the ones who leave everything), and yet in health you proclaim *Praise to the Lord*; in sickness, *Praise to the Lord*; when admired, *Praise to the Lord*; when one criticizes, scorns you, *Praise to the Lord*—or whether you walk on the Path fully involved with and in the world of forms and desires: *I want the concave, but I know there will be the convex. One item of good news, okay. One piece of bad news, okay. I succeed, okay. There is an obstacle, okay.* Whether you take everything, or you take nothing because "*I am beyond*"...truth is sharp. *But this is* not *my truth today;*

I am not *beyond. I still want to avoid a disagreeable situation; I still want to be done with another type of situation.* In the latter approach you welcome *everything* with equanimity. And this attitude will be effective in transforming you inwardly in the spiritual sense, in the sense of liberty.

❧

There are two possibilities: whether your commitment to an activity, whatever it may be, makes you forget the Indestructible all the time; or, contrarily, whether your commitment to a relative human undertaking makes you remember it. All of what interests you, pleases you, displeases you, attracts you, repulses you, produces in you a happy emotion or a painful emotion—all of it, rather than making you forgetful, can remind you unceasingly of what is Essential. And with reflection and conviction, you will see that it is possible.

In the well-known "Our Father" prayer there is this demand: "Lead us not into temptation." In Latin, the believer recites this prayer this way. Why would God lead us into temptation while asking us not to fail? Less confusing translations have been proposed: "Do not submit us to temptation," "Do not let us fail before temptation." Let's consider that this world, with its beautiful sides and its ugly sides—at least according to us—is God's creation or, from another metaphysical view, the expression of God, the dance of God, like waves are the dance of the ocean (*ex nihilo* creation or *ex Deo* creation). Now, this world—which in principle God created and animates—is a constant temptation to forgetting this omnipresent God. God is in the background of all that happens—happiness/unhappiness, success/failure, arrival/departure, birth/death—but this world of appearances is full of constant temptation to forget what is essential. The issue is not the temptation to cheat on one's wife, nor the temptation to not be honest in business—all these temptations having to do with morality—but the temptation to forget the Absolute. I refer to "God," even if His Name is not part of Swâmiji's vocabulary, because, for you, it is a better-known word than *atman*. Hear it as "Ultimate Reality" or the "Divine," as Hindus say. This daily world is a permanent temptation to forgetting, and thus is a world of sleep: problems, difficulties, success, the smile of a man, the gaze of a woman. What is destructible always makes you forget what is Indestructible.

Your one possibility to really change your level of *being* is to come to the point that this relative world does not distract you anymore from what is Essential. "Do not lead us into temptation" implies: *This world, which is Your work, Your creation, Your manifestation, makes me forget You all throughout my days.* But a conversion is possible: *This world, which is Your work, will make me remember You all the time.* In a Trappist monastery, everything is organized in order that the monk or the nun remembers from morning till night: the architecture, recitation of the Offices, prayer in the working place. It is the same in a Zen monastery. *But for us, we live in this world in which all is organized in order that we forget what is Essential; and the key is to come to the point where what is impermanent reminds us unceasingly of the Eternal.*

This key is simple. It is the objective statement of (recognition of) the reaction that takes place in and imposes itself on you. You are aware enough to acknowledge that an emotion has just been triggered in you, whether it appears to you as negative or positive. And with enduring practice, you are aware enough to connect it, each time, to the remembrance of the Great Goal and of your commitment to the Path. Think, digest, and assimilate this fundamental idea: *Ah! an emotion: remember, remember.* Today, the emotion tells you: Forget, forget, let yourself be completely carried away by your happy overexcitement; let yourself be completely carried away by your fury. You can create, if you really want it, a new connection within you: *I remember.* This is completely feasible if you just give thought to the fundamental ideas, and experience and check their value.

By such remembrance, you benefit yourself on both sides: in your so-called ordinary existence and in your search for the inner Kingdom. It is this world of the ephemeral that becomes the support for your progression towards the Eternal. If you do not come to this reconciliation, your process is without end. On the one hand, there will be fascinating books to read, a precious week spent nearby a sage...and the rest of the time you will be completely taken again by old mechanisms.

"Keep awake all of the time...and pray unceasingly." (Matt. 26:40; 1 Thess. 5:17) How will you manage to watch and pray unceasingly if this world makes you forget to pray and watch from morning till night? How will you come to the point where each incident in this relative world makes you contrarily remember to watch and pray? Either it is *that* or it is nothing. And attempting to practice merely from time to time, especially when you are very unhappy, is not a full commitment on the Path.

Yes, an emotion arose in you. Ego has been touched and did react. But this is an occasion for practicing. Not *Me, furious;* nor *Me, desperate;* but what Swâmiji called, "You yourself in your own intrinsic dignity." Me all excited when everything goes right, or me distraught when everything goes wrong is not me in my own intrinsic dignity. Here and now, try to come back to a more central presence to yourself, like the axis about which a pendulum swings, the axis with no contrary. Observe the motion of the pendulum within you: I notice a happy emotion; I notice a negative emotion—i.e., an emotion founded on a No. *Through practice, what makes you forget will make you remember.* That practice will not perform some miracle from one day to the next, and you will not be "settled in Brahman" forever, but this is what you are called to. And this core daily practice will lead you to the Great Goal.

Remember Swâmi Prajnânpad's words: "Everything which comes to you comes to you as a challenge and as an opportunity." Do you practice, or do you let yourself be carried away by reaction? There is emotion...so you aren't anymore situated in the axis, but carried away to one side or the other. Come back to yourself! *I am a musical instrument, slightly or seriously out of tune, so I do not go on playing. I first tune the instrument.* Emotions...you will experience some of them for a long time, but this does not matter, for as soon as an emotion shows up, you will inwardly do what you've got to do. Inner fires will go on starting in you, but you will still have the extinguisher close at hand. Hear this: *Changes of mood—even if you have already progressed much and found great success in practice—will go on being triggered in you.* Something touches you positively and here comes a happy emotion. Happy emotion is surely welcomed in the moment, but it is only the opposite of painful emotion. If you are free from the power that criticism has to hurt you, you have to be free from the power that compliments have to please you. There is a completely different way to be happy than by experiencing happy emotions. But even when you have progressed quite far, there will be times when you will still be carried away. Dare to hear this, and do not fall into the trap of deception: *Here we go, once again I am unhappy, once again I am discouraged!* With this in your mind, the idea remains, *Life makes me suffer, again.* No, life is as it is. A piece of information, a fact, an event produces in you a painful reaction; don't be surprised. But don't waste three seconds being identified with the reaction. Rather, *I see and I recognize.*

In order for a reaction to vanish, you will discover an ability (and this is *actually* possible) to let this reaction be dissolved, to *live* the emotion, to not be fooled by your thoughts, and to merely remember. In fact, this is the *only* thing you have to remember: that if there is an emotion, you no longer "see," but you invent a world. With such invention you then have to say, "Yes, it is" to a terrible world, when in fact the "terrible" is yours. While observing yourself with awareness, you will discover that you immediately gave a threatening, painful, annoying value to some fact, whereas the fact itself was neutral. There really is a rope, but you have mistaken it for a snake. This is an appearance. You isolate a part from the whole, like a forward zoom on a camera isolates a detail in the whole of the reality, a detail in the whole of your existence. You give a fact a negative value that it does not really have. From that, the fact that was minor becomes enormous, and rather than having to accept the reality of the minor fact, you are then compelled to accept a tragic fact that you created yourself. It is you who, by your immediate response, "No," have made of it something so worrisome. If from a boil you make a skin cancer, will you attempt as a heroic disciple to accept that you have skin cancer? From a bit of bad news you made something very heavy and threatening for the future. These are only thoughts; this is only the cruel play of your own mind.

"All makes me remember the practice": This is what we have to come to! If not, you may read interesting books, you may be satisfied by a seminar, your heart may be touched by the beautiful gaze of a sage in a photo, but you will not change. There are times when all of this becomes very concrete: *I roll up my sleeves. I take a pickaxe to dig the ground, a shovel to remove it, and at some point I have a hole in front of me to plant my little maple tree.* The good news is that someday this maple tree will be twelve meters high and eight meters wide, or, as the Gospels say, will become such a large tree that all the birds of the sky will come to make their nests in it.

❧

Practice! It is true that the Kingdom of Heaven is already within you, just as nudity is not in the future but is already present, covered by our clothes. The very idea of practicing and progressing from this viewpoint may be questioned by teachings that affirm you are either awake or not, that's it; that in the state of non-awakening, the idea of progression is an illusion. But all of the Buddhist literature—*hinayana, mahayana, tantrayana*—is based on practicing and training in order that, some day, you indeed go beyond. This is what Swâmiji summarized in the words, "Revolution is the culmination of evolution." So practice. One practices piano; one trains oneself. "Asceticism" in Greek means "training." It was the word that was used about the athletes who trained themselves for the famous Athenian Olympic games.

You train to transform your relationship to others and to yourself. But do you really have the intention to listen to others, or in reality is it that you don't really want to listen and prefer to remain shut down within your own thoughts? Theoretically, you know that to *really listen* to others is part of the opening of the heart and the intellect. It means including, comprehending, creating non-separation with others. But what about when the other tells you for the hundredth time the thing that you consider is wrong and represents merely his or her own mind? *In reality, to attempt here-and-now communion with this person is the Path towards non-duality.* "Me only; me and others; others and me; others only" was the progression taught by Swâmiji. The ego vanishes while welcoming and getting larger and larger.[2] Are you decided, yes or no, to practice communion with others here and now, whatever they may say, and even if you consider that they are wrong?

If a practice proposed to you does not really inspire you, it is obvious that you will make nothing of it. If you have in mind to play

---

[2]   *Welcoming* in the sense of saying Yes to what is; *getting larger and larger,* meaning that ego comes into communion with each manifestation of the whole universe, and thus it dissolves.

the guitar well, you will practice. If you have in mind to develop the same muscles as Arnold Schwarzenegger, you will do weightlifting every evening after work. If you feel only, *Maybe I should...I'd rather... but I'm not really motivated,* look for something else that motivates you in the whole of what the teaching proposes to you. There is no risk of being wrong if what motivates you is at least a part of the Path.

Now let's suppose that you feel, *I really want to be in communion with the other*—beyond *he upsets me...she doesn't understand.* The first step is to see your own impediments to really listening to and being in communion with the other. You will discover how much you are caught in your own thoughts. And when you are harassed by your own thoughts, the other has to say really interesting things to get your attention. If you really want to be in "non-duality" with the other, here and now—which will allow you to be free from your own limitations and to progress on the Path—then *practice as if there were no impediment.* What do you want? To no longer react in anger? Practice not reacting in anger anymore. Meanwhile, notice that discontent or non-loving emotions will still arise in you. The intent is not to judge yourself but to understand yourself. Practicing *as if* there were no impediment is what was proposed to us as children. But only half of the practice was given to us: "You must not lie, you must not do this, you must not have bad thoughts, you must love your little brother"...whom you continued to hate! We were told what we had to do, but not how to do it. It was totally insufficient.

Place "listening to the other" as an essential element in your approach to the whole Path. Not only, *I should listen to the other for the other's sake.* Of course, he or she would be happy to feel welcomed with such attention and love. But also do it for yourself. All you do for the other, you also do for yourself; not in the sense of doing it *for* ego but in order to *transcend* ego. You cannot listen to another if you are preoccupied with your own difficulties. How could you be interested in someone else when you yourself have such a need to be understood and listened to? So...how to free yourself little by little from your own needs in order to be available to others? You practice as if there were no obstacle, but you see your failures. You observe these failures and you question, *Why can't I?*

I want to succeed in loving my enemies. Say that someone exhibits hostile behavior towards you, and you merely consider the appearance of things. The appearance is that someone is unfriendly towards you. But you must look deeper than or beyond appearances. Someone tells you that another person spoke harsh and very scornful words about you, and someone else confirms that. You want to succeed in having only love for the person who talked badly about you, but this is not at all part of your mechanicality! Your mechanicality is to react, is to be angry with him. So will you try to understand what keeps you prisoner of your own world? Watch and you will see. One has to work on these impediments, these obstacles, to be cured. *I am not capable of welcoming the other for I am way too much, today, preoccupied by me, me, me.* How can we be at once very preoccupied with ourselves and very open to others? There is long-term, inner transformation work to do. This is not mysterious. One would like to have keys, secrets, a very fast technique: You have a fever, the doctor gives you antibiotics, five days later you are healed. This is true medicine! But I never saw such a thing in ashrams and monasteries where I stayed in the past.

You will see deeper than the surface if you are first *in communion with* the surface. Yes, in one sense whatever occurs is sacred, for this is *what is* here and now. Many times I heard Swâmiji saying, "Everything is neutral," and I had difficulty in understanding this. But Swâmiji also said, "Everything is neutral and so is sacred." *Sacred* because *it is* (isness, suchness, thatness)...here and now; what happens happens. He or she speaks to me in such and such a way. Yes! And "the other" is the very ground you can walk on to get free from yourself. Liberation is being rid of the burden of oneself: *Me, they don't understand. Me, I am admired. Me, nobody even looks at me. Me, I'm getting old....Me...Me.* To be free from oneself is what some traditions have called "death to oneself." Free from oneself and available to the other! This does not mean that if the other laboriously explains to you that 3 times 9 equals 30 you will be convinced of it. The other may say what is technically non-truth, but what is sacred is that this person, here and now, says that.

By admitting these ideas you will attain access to the depth. What truly underlies this world that we unceasingly qualify as good or bad? We unceasingly grab what pleases us and reject what does not. *Non-me*, whatever it may be, is our best ground to walk on towards liberation *from me*. And this is what ego does not want to hear. To ego, the other has to fulfill *my* expectations. The other has to make *me* happy and not spoil *my* life. If we understand that this self-centeredness is the prison, the fundamental spiritual pathology, then the other—the first "enemy"—will become a precious help. Just now—and this is often true within coupled relationships, which hold an important place in some people's existences—here and now, the other *does not* fulfill *my* expectations. So on the human plane, *I may lose*, but on the Divine level, *I may be a winner*. You use as a springboard towards the "Self" what at the ordinary level is purely and merely suffering.

Let's imagine (I will take a well-known and concrete example) a man who wants very much to make love, though his wife is not ready for that at this moment. From a human point of view this is totally frustrating. There arises a suffering, a demand, a reproach. Humanly, you are a loser—you feel the desire to make love and your wife is not at all situated on this wavelength. If you are not a disciple, there is only frustration. If you are a disciple, you remember what has been taught: *Humanly, I'm losing, it is true; but Divinely, I want to win.* If you succeed in every circumstance in supporting yourself by accepting *what is* (in letting the future free, you will see what decisions will have to be made), frustration will be transformed into peace and serenity. Do not reduce this to the example of the sexual availability of your partner. Opportunities like this are available every day. With such practice you may enter into another level and into contact—like two electric wires—with a depth within yourself that is here, which has always and untiringly waited for you.

I am not pleading the "other's" cause. I am pleading yours. This is about *you*, your progression. How many times did I hear, "Why is it always *my turn* to practice? Couldn't you convince my wife to do it?" "Why must *I* take my medicines in the morning? Could my wife take *hers* sometimes?" You have this thought in the background of your mind: that if your wife practiced what *she* has been taught, she would become exactly what *you* want her to become. *She will be like me, for I am right. If she practices, she will think like me...!*

I am not pleading the "other's" cause. While it will be good for the other—whoever he or she may be—to feel themselves being listened to, understood, recognized, it will be even more precious for you. Always remember Swâmiji's words: "All that comes to you, comes to you as a challenge and as an opportunity." What happens to me is happening to me, not to my neighbor! *What happens to me is my own lot so there is no need for me to be unceasingly analyzing and discussing it* (which is like telling God that He is wrong with me). It is not *you* who are being deported to China by the Chinese—those are Tibetan lamas. It is not *you* who are in a wheelchair—it is one of your friends who had a bad car accident. You know the formula: All that comes to you comes to you because you attracted it. I recognize that this corresponds to me.

But the most precious thing is that all that comes to you comes as "a challenge and an opportunity." *All.* The challenge is, Do I practice? Yes or no? Will you react as you did before in some way, like everybody else? *I'm not happy, I get nervous, I'm carried away, I*

indulge in the most crazy and petty thoughts. Yet still, there is a challenge
. . . and an opportunity! You have to hear this word "opportunity"
in an extremely positive way, fully happy, recognizing that here, in
this, is the external and precious support that I need in order to
inwardly get in contact with my own peace, in the depths. I say
it again: *Humanly, at the usual level of the mind, of ego, of attraction
and repulsion, you are the loser.* But at another level, you may be an
immediate winner—not "when I'm done with my psychotherapy" or
"when I'll have completely changed."

When you *have* changed a lot, then whatever intense effort
is asked of you today will become much easier, the same as with
whatever art one practices. "Opportunity" is a very positive word.
You can also substitute the word "chance." The "other," at the very
moment when his or her attitude is negative towards you, becomes
your most precious opportunity/chance to enter into contact with
God within you. You may replace the word "God" with "atman" or
"Buddha nature" if this is more inspiring to you.

In each aspect or example of existence, the whole Path, the
whole teaching is contained: the ego, the mind, duality, attraction
and repulsion, time, causality. All the universal issues are also found
in the smallest examples, not only in those that involve strong
emotions and not only in moments of bliss or deep meditation. A
new approach consists of deciding with the whole of your being, *I no
longer discuss reality (with a small "r"). The way the usual world appears
here and now is an expression of Ultimate Reality, as each wave is an
expression of the one ocean.*

Swâmi Prajnânpad also pronounced these astonishing words:
"As long as you do not realize that what is pleasant and what is
unpleasant does not exist at all, you cannot get free from them." What
is unpleasant—one could also say "unfavorable"—is the situation
in which you are humanly losing. But if you are metaphysically
winning, you can't say that it is unfortunate. What is unpleasant is the

usual experience. If you are fiercely criticized, this is part of what is unpleasant, and if you are approved and thanked, this is part of what is pleasant. But the fact that one is crushing you with reproaches is *support for* a moment of awakening. *You use what is unfavorable to get into contact with what is beyond the ordinary favorable and unfavorable.*

What is commonly pleasant encourages us to easily forget our commitment to the Path. This is well known. One remembers God more when all goes badly than when all goes well. When you catch yourself in the mood of ordinary happy emotion and you know that this joyful mood is momentary, you know that what appears today to you as so advantageous will have consequences you ignore and have no control over tomorrow. *Today,* this *is happening to me; tomorrow,* that *will happen to me.* On the other hand, from something "bad," sometimes something "good" comes. You will discover that reality is neutral, and that it is we who qualify it in the moment as "good" or "bad." This *is,* so it is sacred. It is a challenge and an opportunity. When we are totally convinced, it is not a challenge anymore, for we are no longer able to not practice here and now. Then what seems to harm us becomes the perfect help in fostering in us a happy state; but that happiness is different from what is usually pleasant, usually opposed to what is painful.

About that, I want to quote some other surprising words of Swâmiji's: "As long as whatever *exists* for you, you cannot be free from it." You are free from what does not exist at all for you, what is not part of your world, what plays no part in your existence. While we may know that "it exists," still it does not exist *to us.* If something called "success" in the mundane sense of the word *exists* to you, which means that it is important in your eyes, you cannot be free of it. You will then consider every event of your existence according to the fact that it either assists or prevents this success. If this idea completely disappears as a personal interest—a hermit in his cave is not preoccupied by success—then are you free.

The Path leads you towards autonomy and non-dependence. By finding plenitude, joy, and peace at the core of yourself, you become more and more free from slavery to fears and desires. But I know this absolute detachment may appear more *in*human than *super*human to ego. Do not reject either the idea or the possibility of this type of detachment—or a progressive unfolding of it. It is not about renunciation or sacrifice, but about going beyond. Between the ages of ten and thirteen, roller skating was very important to me (the only physical activity I was good at). Then naturally it disappeared from my existence. Between thirteen and sixteen I was passionate about fishing and hunting, and I knew by heart the then-famous catalog of "Manufrance" (firearms and bicycle factory). That page was then turned, and I went on to something else: classical theater and the *Comedie-Française's* actors (*the one* classical theater in Paris).

Swâmiji would blow on the embers that were under the ashes in order to ignite flames; thus all that was hidden in us would come to the surface. In some cases, a little blow was enough to kindle a big fire within three seconds. One day Swâmiji told me, "You could do politics, becoming a member of parliament. Yes, yes, you studied Political Science; one has to be able to talk before people in order to convince them. And Denise[3] told that you were very gifted in lecturing..." Thus Swâmiji blew for one hour on ashes, but there was not the least ember under them. On the other hand, all that concerned women *did exist* for me. Success too was very important at a certain time. But politics, never! It was something that was not part of my world.

I know that for some people "it exists" to gamble in casinos and to lose. Some need therapy to heal from the madness of gambling. I never ever enter a casino, never put a dime in a slot machine.

---

[3]   Arnaud's first wife.

Gambling and casinos are also realities that never existed for me. But as long as something still exists for you, you cannot be free of it. You remain enslaved to successes and failures, to the opposition between good and bad or good and evil, according to your assessment in the moment.

But I must also tell you that "something"—something which is not minor—will continue to concern "you," even if the "me" does vanish: the suffering of others. May you be inspired towards your personal victory over your own suffering by contributing to reducing the unhappiness around you.

Don't be impatient. Be faithful to yourself day by day, step by step. Look very far away on the horizon, towards where and to what you are going. And look very closely at yourself, at where you are just placing your feet, step by step.

INDEX

Index

145